MW00954967

IRON IN

PLANTFOODS

A Complete Guide to Increasing Iron
Consumption with a Plant-Based Diet,
Roots, Shoots, and Superfoods

By
Ella Furry

Copyright 2023 by Ella Furry All rights reserved. Except for reviewers who may cite brief sections in reviews, no part of this book may be duplicated in any way, by any electronic or mechanical means, including information storage and retrieval systems, without the publisher's prior written consent.

Copyright © 2023

Table of Contents

Foreword

Getting Around Unknown Waters: An Introduction to Untraveled Paths

The whispers at the beginning of a book, the foreword, have an odd power. These are maps with hints of the adventures to come, etched with anticipation. This time, dear reader, you are about to embark on an unknown journey into the limitless potential that is inside of you.

This book is neither a strict itinerary nor a compass. Rather, it is like a lantern thrown upon the glistening ocean of your own potential. Instead of dogmatic declarations, you will find invitations to investigate, to think critically, and to kindle the spark of your own special potential within these pages.

Think of it as a tapestry made by both known and unknown hands using threads from a variety of experiences. It is filled to the brim with tales of victories and setbacks, of paths traveled and not traveled, whispering not of absolutes but of the thrilling uncertainty that permeates every genuine journey.

Forget for a second the well-worn expectation maps. Dispatch the predestined paths that other people have planned for you. This book is a siren song, a call to the explorer inside of you, inviting you to set your own path beneath the big, ever-changing sky of your own potential.

Get ready to hear viewpoints that startle you out of the comfort of the known, voices that both challenge and inspire. Get ready for epiphanies, when the earth moves beneath your feet and the horizon appears farther than you could have ever dreamed.

This is not a trip for the easily discouraged. It is a journey through uncharted territory and an exploration of the unknown. There will be times when you feel scared, doubtful, and frustrated. However, these difficulties are what will eventually bring about your biggest changes.

Now, my dear reader, inhale deeply and climb aboard this literary ship. Allow the whispers of these pages to lead you towards your infinite potential rather than a preset destination. Let the wind of curiosity fill your sails.

The purpose of this book is to ignite the questions that will illuminate your own unique path, not to provide answers. It's a call to release the shackles of expectation, claim the thrilling freedom of your own unfolding story, and embrace the messy, exciting beauty of becoming.

Let these pages' ink serve as a compass rather than a map. Let the tales serve as embers rather than solutions. And allow the voyage to be solely yours, my dear reader.

Introduction

Uncovering the Tapestry: An Overview of Unexplored Frontiers

Imagine experience, knowledge, and imagination woven together to create a colorful and complex tapestry. The strong, stable warp stands for the pillars of your existence, the things that hold you in place. Your journey's ever-changing threads, decisions, and paths are embodied by the weft, which is dynamic and fluid.

This book is a call to explore this very tapestry, dear reader. It serves as a doorway to unexplored areas within yourself and as a spark for discovering lost connections and incorporating fresh ones into your life's tapestry.

Forget the regimented routines and the white, clinical walls of convention. This journey explores the vibrant bazaar of possibilities, where imagination serves as the compass and curiosity as the currency. Here, the symphony of your own particular potential overpowers dogmas and absolutes like whispers in the wind.

You won't find a set schedule or predetermined locations in these pages. Rather, you will meet a chorus of voices, both known and unknown, and a kaleidoscope of viewpoints. Be ready to have your preconceptions challenged and to be pushed outside of your comfort zone.

Consider this book as a mirror that will show you the rainbow of possibilities within rather than your present reflection. The narratives that you come across are not just stories; rather, they are coals that are just waiting to catch fire inside of you.

Preparedly face the uncertainties and fears that impede your progress, the shadows that lurk in the corners of your life story. But don't give up because the seeds of your biggest changes are hidden in these shadows. Accept the darkness, as it is the birthplace of the brightest stars.

This is no journey to be undertaken lightly. It is an ascent up mist-covered peaks and a journey through uncharted territory. There will be periods of uncertainty, annoyance, and complete disorientation. Let these moments serve as your guides and instructors as you navigate the winding paths of self-discovery, though.

For these missteps harbor the seeds of perseverance, the determination to carve out your own route, to change the course of your life. Recall, reader, that the hardest ascents frequently lead to the most magnificent vistas.

So inhale deeply, stifle your inner critic, and venture out on this literary journey. Allow your curiosity to take you where you've never gone before, and let the pages of this tapestry point you in the direction of your own limitless potential.

This book is a compass, not a map. It is a question rather than an answer. And you alone, dear reader, are on this journey.

Let the tapestry unfold, turn the page now, and start the thrilling dance of becoming.

- **Why Iron Matters: An Essential Mineral for Health and Welfare**

Despite its apparent simplicity, iron is a very complex and important element for our health. This vital mineral powers our cells and shapes our lives in ways we frequently take for granted. It makes up about 4% of our body weight and is woven into the very fabric of our existence.

The Transporter of Oxygen: The primary function of iron is in the transport of oxygen. Hemoglobin, a protein found embedded in red blood cells, functions as a taxi driver, carrying oxygen vital to life from our lungs to every part of our body. Our organs, brains, and muscles are continuously fueled by this flow, which keeps them operating at their best. This oxygen delivery system malfunctions in the absence of enough iron, resulting in exhaustion, dyspnea, and a variety of other health issues.

Past the Blood: The effects of iron go far beyond oxygen. Myoglobin, a protein found in muscle cells that stores oxygen for sudden bursts of activity, depends on it for proper function. It is essential for the synthesis of DNA, enzyme activity, and energy production. Iron has an impact on our immune system as well, helping it to fight off infections and maintain optimal function.

The dilemma of deficiency: Regretfully, billions of people worldwide suffer from iron deficiency, which is one of the most prevalent nutritional deficiencies, especially in women and children. Wide-ranging effects include impaired physical and cognitive growth, decreased productivity at work, and an increased risk of complications during pregnancy and childbirth.

Plant-Based Conundrum: A person switching to a plant-based diet may have concerns about their iron levels. Although meat is frequently promoted as the main source of iron, the reality is much more complex. Even though plant-based sources typically contain less iron per serving, non-heme iron, which is the type of iron they do contain, can still be absorbed just as well with the right dietary practices.

Opening the Iron Powerhouse of Plants: Knowing how iron interacts with other nutrients is essential to optimizing iron absorption from plant-based sources. Vitamin C, which is abundant in peppers and citrus fruits, is a powerful enhancer that helps the body absorb iron. Similarly, adding turmeric or beta-carotene (**found in leafy greens and carrots**) to meals high in iron can enhance absorption even more.

A Harmony of Elements: Creating a well-rounded and varied plant-based diet is the best way to ensure that you are consuming the most iron possible. Iron-rich foods include legumes like beans and lentils, leafy greens like spinach and kale, whole grains like quinoa and oats, and nuts and seeds like cashews and pumpkin seeds. Iron is guaranteed to reach its intended location when consumed in harmony with other nutrients by combining these foods with fruits and vegetables that are high in vitamin C.

Beyond the Plate: Although nutrition is important, iron absorption can also be impacted by other factors. Iron bioavailability, for instance, can be impacted by cooking techniques. Iron can be preserved by using softer cooking techniques like steaming or simmering as opposed to intense boiling.

Furthermore, iron absorption may be hampered by specific drugs and medical disorders, so it's crucial to speak with a doctor if you have any concerns.

Encouraging Plant-Based Decisions In the end, knowing the importance of iron and how abundant it is in plants gives us the confidence to adopt a plant-based diet. We can guarantee our bodies have the iron they require to flourish by including foods high in iron, learning about absorption boosters, and getting help when necessary. This will pave the way for health, vitality, and a sustainable future.

Thus, keep in mind the silent strength of iron operating in the background the next time you reach for a plate of delicious plant-based food. This vital mineral, which permeates every mouthful, powers our bodies, feeds our cells, and ultimately molds our lives.

- ## The Importance of Iron for Plant-Based Diets: Establishing Health from the Foundation Up

For a lot of people adopting a plant-based diet, iron is a major concern. This essential mineral, which has historically been connected to meat, frequently raises questions regarding intake and absorption. But a deeper examination reveals an unexpected fact: plant-based diets can be just as successful as animal diets in giving our bodies the iron they need, if not more so. Comprehending the significance of iron and the distinct obstacles and prospects associated with plant-based sources endows us with the ability to construct robust health from the foundation up.

The Symphony of Iron: Iron is a multipurpose conductor that plays a symphony of essential functions in our cells. It transports oxygen from the lungs to the tissues via hemoglobin, enabling all of our bodily functions and mental processes. It is also essential for the synthesis of DNA, the production of energy, the operation of enzymes, and the regulation of our immune system and metabolism. This essential orchestra goes silent in the absence of enough iron, resulting in exhaustion, weakness, and impaired cognitive function.

The Landscape of Plant-Based Iron: Even though meat has a higher iron content per serving, there are a wide variety of iron-rich foods found in the kingdom of plants. Supreme among legumes, such as beans, lentils, and chickpeas, are rich sources of non-heme iron that are just waiting to be absorbed. Whole grains like quinoa and oats, nuts and seeds like pumpkin and sesame seeds, and leafy greens like kale and spinach all join the chorus, contributing their own special iron-rich qualities.

Unlocking the Absorption Potential: Understanding absorption is essential to making the most of this abundant supply of iron derived from plants. Non-heme iron from plants has more difficulties than heme iron from meat. But nature offers creative allies to help us get over these obstacles. Iron is bound to vitamin C, the brilliant conductor of absorption that can be found in citrus fruits and peppers, which facilitates iron's easy passage into our cells. The master of vibrant veggies like carrots and leafy greens, beta-carotene, along with the pungent spice turmeric, enhance the bioavailability of iron.

The Skill of Arranging Meals: Creating an iron-rich plant-based diet is a team effort rather than a solo endeavor. A nutrient symphony is produced when iron-rich foods are paired with their absorption enhancers, optimizing the benefits of every bite. A few dishes from this culinary concerto are a bowl of leafy greens tossed with a little turmeric, a quinoa salad dressed in a zesty vinaigrette, and a lentil stew full of vitamin C-rich tomatoes and bell peppers. Past the Plate: Iron absorption is influenced by a number of factors in addition to dietary strategies. Simmering or steaming are gentler cooking techniques that do not damage the iron molecule as much as boiling does. Absorption may also be hampered by specific drugs and medical disorders, so it's crucial to get advice from a healthcare provider.

Encouraging Plant-Based Decisions With knowledge of the significance of iron and the distinct benefits of plant-based sources, we can confidently adopt a diet and lifestyle abundant in this essential mineral. By adding a variety of foods high in iron, using absorption enhancers, and getting educated advice, we can create a health symphony inside our bodies. This gives us the ability to contribute to a more just and sustainable food system in addition to helping us thrive on a plant-based diet.

Thus, let's toast to iron—both in its classic form and in its colorful plant-based form. One delectable bite at a time, we can create a symphony of health by comprehending its function and realizing its potential.

- **Uncovering the Secrets of Your Plant-Powered Body: An Understanding of Iron Absorption**

The invisible conductor of our biological orchestra, iron, is essential for producing energy, sustaining general health, and moving oxygen around the body. Although we frequently link iron with meat, the kingdom of plants has a rich and varied repertoire of iron-rich treasures that are just waiting for our bodies to absorb and utilize them. But the secret to realizing the full benefits of a plant-based diet is to grasp the subtleties of iron absorption.

The Two Faces of Iron: Heme and non-heme are the two primary forms of iron. Our bodies are capable of easily absorbing heme iron, which is mostly found in meat. The journey of non-heme iron, which is prevalent in plants, is a little more complicated. Although our bodies are capable of absorbing non-heme iron, it takes some coordination to get the job done.

The Absorption Enhancers: Iron requires a supporting cast to function at its best, just like any other good conductor. This is where vitamin C's magic comes into play. Ascorbic acid functions as an encouraging agent by attaching itself to non-heme iron and allowing it to enter our intestinal cells more easily. Consider it as dissolving the iron into a form that is easily absorbed. Broccoli, bell peppers, and citrus fruits like oranges, grapefruits, and peppers are all excellent providers of this important vitamin C.

The Supporting Cast: Other nutrients are just as important to the iron absorption symphony as vitamin C. The mastermind behind vibrant veggies like carrots and leafy greens, beta-carotene, adds to the chorus by promoting the transformation of non-heme iron into a form that is easier to absorb. Turmeric, an aromatic spice, contributes its own melody in the meantime and may help reduce inflammation, which can hinder the absorption of iron.

The Harmony of Food Pairing: Putting together a delicious, well-balanced plant-based diet is like writing a masterpiece of culinary arts. Maximizing iron intake requires matching foods high in iron with their absorption enhancers. A lentil stew that is cooked with tomatoes and bell peppers is a vitamin C and iron symphony. A quinoa salad with chopped red pepper and zest of citrus satisfies all the cravings. And a harmonious combination of iron and absorption boosters is created when a bowl of leafy greens is tossed with a dressing infused with turmeric.

Beyond the Plate: Although dietary approaches play a major role in iron absorption, other factors may also impact the play's outcome. Simmering and steaming are gentler cooking techniques that do not damage the iron molecule as much as boiling does. Iron absorption may also be impacted by specific drugs and medical conditions, so it's crucial to get advice from a healthcare provider.

Encouraging Plant-Based Decisions: We can boldly adopt a plant-based lifestyle high in this essential mineral by knowing the nuances of iron absorption and the plethora of options found in the plant kingdom. By consuming a variety of foods, combining them in inventive ways, and receiving knowledgeable advice, we can fully utilize plant-powered iron and create a body symphony of health and wellbeing.

Let irony's music fill your plate, then! If you have a little knowledge and a lot of imagination, you can make sure that your plant-based diet provides your body with the iron it needs to thrive. Recall that iron's power comes from both its presence and absorption. With the abundance of the plant kingdom, you can unlock a world of vibrant health and well-being by knowing the supporting cast and planning your meals with intention.

Part 1:

A Comprehensive Look at Iron, the Super Mineral for a Plant-Based Diet

Iron, which is frequently connected to red meat, may be a concern for people switching to a plant-based diet. But worry not! Iron-rich treasures abound in the kingdom of plants, just waiting to be discovered and utilized by our bodies. Let's take a closer look at iron requirements, including how it affects our health, how to absorb it as much as possible, and how to create a plant-based, high-iron diet.

Iron: The Conductor of the Oxygen Orchestra

Consider the iron that serves as the conductor of the essential oxygen transportation system within your body as a busy metropolis. Iron is a component of red blood cells that transport oxygen from the lungs to tissues, giving each cell the energy it needs to survive. This seemingly straightforward action affects everything from energy levels to cognitive performance, which is why iron is a crucial component of our overall health.

Plant-Based Iron Superpower: Dispelling the Myth About Meat

Although meat has a higher iron content per serving, there are a wide variety of iron-rich plant options available. Beans, lentils, and chickpeas are the ultimate legumes because they are a great source of non-heme iron, which our bodies can easily absorb when we use the proper techniques. Adding their distinct notes of iron, leafy greens like kale and spinach, whole grains like quinoa and oats, and nuts and seeds like pumpkin and sesame seeds all join the chorus.

Unlocking Absorption Potential: The Symphony of Support Found in Nature

Non-heme iron from plants must go through a slightly more difficult absorption process than heme iron from meat. But worry not—nature offers a nutrient-rich supporting cast to help clear the path. Citrus fruits and peppers contain vitamin C, a bright conductor of absorption that binds to iron to facilitate its uptake by intestinal cells. The mastermind behind vibrant veggies like carrots and leafy greens, beta-carotene, steps in to improve iron bioavailability. Turmeric is an aromatic spice that adds a distinct melody and may help reduce inflammation, which can hinder absorption.

Constructing a Steel-Rich Symphony on Your Dish

Consider your meals to be harmonious culinary compositions consisting of both iron-rich foods and absorption enhancers. A lentil stew that is cooked with tomatoes and bell peppers is a vitamin C and iron symphony. A quinoa salad with chopped red pepper and zest of citrus satisfies all the cravings. And a harmonious combination of iron and absorption boosters is created when a bowl of leafy greens is tossed with a dressing infused with turmeric.

Beyond the Plate: Achieving Your Specific Needs in Iron Absorption Optimization

Although diet plans are important, keep in mind that everybody is different. Simmering and steaming are gentler cooking techniques that do not damage the iron molecule as much as boiling does. Iron absorption may also be impacted by specific drugs and medical conditions, so it's crucial to get advice from a healthcare provider.

Encouraging Plant-Based Decisions: Accept Iron with Self-Assurance

You can embrace a vibrant and iron-rich lifestyle with confidence if you know the benefits of plant-based iron and the resources available to you. Your conductors to a symphony of health and well-being are a variety of food options, imaginative pairings, and knowledgeable advice. Thus, let's toast to iron—both in its conventional form and in its varied and mouth watering plant-based form. Recall that the abundance of the plant kingdom can open up a world of iron-powered health for you with a little knowledge and a lot of inventiveness.

Bonus Tip: Because fermented plant foods like miso and tempeh naturally contain probiotics, they can improve the absorption of iron.

The iron essentials are a great place to start your plant-based journey, and never forget that you are the conductor of your own health!

Chapter 1:

Describing Iron: How to Use This Super Mineral in a Plant-Based Diet

Iron is a key player in our health orchestra but is frequently shrouded in mystery. This vital mineral serves as a conductor, carrying oxygen that is necessary for life to every part of our body, and is woven into the structure of our red blood cells. Though iron is usually associated with meat, the kingdom of plants contains a rich and varied symphony of iron-rich treasures that are just waiting to be found and used by those who adopt a plant-based diet. Together, we will debunk the myths surrounding iron, explore its significance, and equip you to create a vibrant, iron-rich plant-based life.

The Oxygen Waltz: The Crucial Role of Iron

Think of your body as a busy city, where each cell requires continuous oxygen flow to function at its best. Hemoglobin contains iron, which drives your oxygen from your lungs to every part of your body. This essential waltz maintains energy production, mental clarity, and general health. The music falters in the absence of enough iron, resulting in exhaustion, weakness, and even complications in pregnancy and childbirth.

Beyond the Myth of Meat: Revealing Iron Powerhouses Made of Plants

Even though meat has a higher iron content per serving, there are a wide variety of iron-rich plant options available. Rich in non-heme iron, legumes such as beans, lentils, and chickpeas take center stage. Adding their distinct notes of iron, leafy greens like spinach and kale, whole grains like quinoa and oats, and nuts and seeds like pumpkin and sesame seeds all join the chorus. Keep in mind that realizing the full potential of this plant-based iron is just as important as quantity.

Revealing the Absorption Boosters: The Supporting Role of Nature

Compared to heme iron, which is found in meat, non-heme iron must travel through a slightly more complicated pathway in order to enter your cells. But worry not—nature offers a nutrient-rich supporting cast to help clear the path. Citrus fruits and peppers contain vitamin C, a bright conductor of absorption that binds to iron to facilitate its uptake by intestinal cells. The mastermind behind vibrant veggies like carrots and leafy greens, beta-carotene, steps in to improve iron bioavailability. Turmeric is an aromatic spice that adds a distinct melody and may help reduce inflammation, which can hinder absorption.

Putting Together a Culinary Symphony: Iron-Rich Plant-Based Dinners

Consider your meals to be harmonious culinary compositions consisting of both iron-rich foods and absorption enhancers. A lentil stew that is cooked with tomatoes and bell peppers is a vitamin C and iron symphony. A quinoa salad with chopped red pepper and zest of citrus satisfies all the cravings. And a harmonious combination of iron and absorption boosters is created when a bowl of leafy greens is tossed with a dressing infused with turmeric. Never forget that originality is essential!

Beyond the Plate: Optimizing for Your Specific Requirements

Although diet plans are important, keep in mind that everybody is different. Simmering and steaming are gentler cooking techniques that do not damage the iron molecule as much as boiling does. Iron absorption may also be impacted by specific drugs and medical conditions, so it's crucial to get advice from a healthcare provider.

Encouraging Plant-Based Decisions: Accept Iron with Self-Assurance

With the knowledge of iron's potential in the plant kingdom and its demystification, you can confidently adopt a vibrant, iron-rich plant-based diet. To create your own health symphony, experiment with different food options, seek professional advice, and try out creative pairings. Recall that you are in charge of your own wellbeing!

Thus, let's toast to iron—not only in its conventional form but also in its varied and mouth watering plant-based form. From the abundance of the plant kingdom, you can unlock a world of iron-powered health with a little knowledge and a lot of creativity. Allow the sound of iron to saturate your life and your plate!

Bonus Tip: Because fermented plant foods like miso and tempeh naturally contain probiotics, they can improve the absorption of iron.

Recall that you are in charge of crafting your plant-based journey. Accept the power of iron, unravel its mysteries, and allow the orchestra of your health to continue!

○ **Enhancers and Inhibitors of Iron Absorption: Creating a Plant-Based Iron Symphony**

Our health is greatly dependent on iron, the oxygen transport system's life-giving conductor. While meat has easily absorbed heme iron, there are a wealth of non-heme iron treasures in the plant kingdom just waiting to be discovered. But optimizing iron absorption in a plant-based diet means knowing the important players who either uplift or depress the iron content.

The Boosters: The Natural Vitamin C Orchestra

The key player in the absorption of iron is vitamin C. This colorful, zesty masterwork binds to non-heme iron and changes it into a form that your intestinal cells can easily absorb. Imagine it as transforming the iron into a tasty, palatable tune. Broccoli, bell peppers, and citrus fruits like oranges and grapefruits are all members of this vital chorus, prepared to add intensity to the iron symphony.

The Ensemble: The Harmonious Combination of Turmeric and Beta-Carotene

The mastermind behind vibrant veggies like carrots and leafy greens, beta-carotene, steps in to help convert non-heme iron into a form that is easier to absorb. The iron molecule is being fine-tuned for maximum absorption, much like a professional musician. The aromatic spice turmeric adds a unique harmony and may help reduce inflammation, which can hinder the absorption of iron. Visualize it as a calming tune that fosters an atmosphere that is conducive to the absorption of iron.

Food Pairing: Crafting a Masterpiece in the Kitchen

Creating an iron-rich plant-based diet is like creating a masterpiece in the kitchen. Maximizing iron intake requires matching foods high in iron with their absorption enhancers. When lentils are cooked with tomatoes and bell peppers, the iron and vitamin C content of the stew becomes harmonious. A quinoa salad topped with chopped red pepper and zest of citrus strikes all the right notes, with each component contributing its own harmony. Never forget that originality is essential! Try out various combinations and allow your creativity to run wild when it comes to cooking.

The Restrictors: Comprehending the Off-Key Element

Certain inhibitors have the ability to muffle the melody, while enhancers amplify the iron symphony. Whole grains, legumes, and nuts contain phytates, which have the ability to bind with iron and reduce its absorption. But these foods can also be made much less phytate-y by soaking, sprouting, and fermenting, which lets the iron melody come through. Tea and coffee, which contain tannins, can also hinder the absorption of iron, so it's best to avoid having them right before or right after meals high in iron.

Enhancing Iron Symphony: Going Beyond the Plate

Your body is an important part of the iron absorption orchestra. Simmering and steaming are gentler cooking techniques that do not damage the iron molecule as much as boiling does. Iron absorption may also be impacted by specific drugs and medical conditions, so it's crucial to get advice from a healthcare provider.

Encouraging Plant-Based Decisions: Accept Iron with Self-Assurance

Knowing what promotes and hinders iron absorption will help you embrace a plant-based diet high in this essential mineral. Examine a variety of food options, try out inventive combinations, and get knowledgeable advice to create your own harmonious blend of health and wellness. Recall that your health is a conductor!

Thus, let's toast to iron—not only in its conventional form but also in its varied and mouth watering plant-based form. From the abundance of the plant kingdom, you can unlock a world of iron-powered health with a little knowledge and a lot of creativity. Allow the sound of iron to saturate your life and your plate!

Bonus Tip: Because fermented plant foods like miso and tempeh naturally contain probiotics, they can improve the absorption of iron.

Recall that you are in charge of crafting your plant-based journey. Recognize the activators and inhibitors, plan your meals, and allow the iron symphony to continue!

○ **Iron Deficiency: Exposing the Covert Crook and Preserving Your Well-being**

The seemingly insignificant element iron is essential to human health because it conducts the oxygen transport system in our red blood cells. However, a silent thief known as iron deficiency appears when iron levels drop. Knowing what it means is essential to protecting our health, particularly when following a plant-based diet.

The Symphony of Iron: Supplying Energy to Our Organs and Cells

Think of your body as a busy city, where each cell requires continuous oxygen flow to function at its best. Hemoglobin contains iron, which functions as the city's delivery drivers, carrying oxygen from your lungs to every part of the body. This essential symphony guarantees the production of energy, mental clarity, and general health.

Iron deficiency and its guidance: The emergence of the silent thief

Iron deficiency develops when blood iron levels drop below ideal levels; it usually does so quietly at first. But the effects can be profound, affecting both our mental and physical well-being.

The Fatigue Symphony: A Listless and Depleted Feeling

Feeling tired is one of the first symptoms. Our bodies struggle to deliver oxygen, leaving us feeling exhausted, lethargic, and devoid of energy—like a city running out of fuel. This may have a major effect on our day-to-day activities, productivity at work, and general well-being.

The Pale Palette: Diminished Immunity and Color Loss

Red blood cell formation is heavily dependent on iron. Lack of it causes the cells to become paler and less effective oxygen carriers. In addition to causing pallor, which is an obvious indicator of iron deficiency, this can impair our immune systems and increase our vulnerability to infections.

The Blurred Symphony: Mood Swings and Cognitive Decline

Iron is necessary for brain function because it affects the synthesis of neurotransmitters and cognitive functions. Memory loss, focus issues, and brain fog can result from an iron deficiency. Additionally, when the brain tries to function at its best, mood swings, irritability, and even depression can happen.

Beyond the Individual: The Significance of Pregnancy and Child Development

Iron deficiency during pregnancy can have detrimental effects on the developing fetus as well as the mother. Premature birth, low birth weight, and developmental delays are among the risks that may increase. It may worsen pre-existing symptoms in mothers and even cause complications.

Revealing the Burglar: Determining Iron Deficiency

The management of iron deficiency requires early detection. Even though symptoms might be subtle, a straightforward blood test can confirm the diagnosis and provide the details required for a successful course of treatment.

Keeping Your Health Safe: Constructing an Iron-Rich Symphony

The favorable tidings? Iron deficiency can be effectively treated, and adopting a plant-based diet can help both prevent and aid in recovery.

How to do it is as follows:

Accept iron-rich plant-based diets: Iron-rich foods include legumes like beans and lentils, leafy greens like spinach and kale, whole grains like quinoa and oats, and nuts and seeds like sesame and pumpkin.

Combine with enhancers of absorption: Citrus fruits and peppers contain vitamin C, which functions as a conductor to help the body absorb iron. Turmeric and beta-carotene, which are found in vibrant vegetables, can also be beneficial.

Cook with intelligence: Iron content is preserved by using gentle cooking techniques like steaming and simmering.

Ask for advice: For specific guidance on managing any underlying conditions, taking iron supplements if necessary, and making dietary adjustments, speak with a healthcare provider.

Boosting Your Plant-Based Adventure: Self-assurance in Each Bite

You can embark on your plant-based journey with confidence if you are aware of iron deficiency and its effects. You can make sure your body has the iron it needs to thrive by including foods high in iron, using absorption boosters, and getting knowledgeable advice. Keep in mind that you are the conductor of your own health symphony; use the power of iron to play it loud and colorful!

Bonus Tip: Because fermented plant foods like miso and tempeh naturally contain probiotics, they can improve the absorption of iron.

Let the celebration of iron-rich health accompany your plant-based journey. Reveal the covert robber, protect your health, and allow the sound of iron to fill your life!

○ Cracking the Iron Mysteries: Identifying and Treating Iron Deficiency

Our bodies and minds are powered by iron, the conductor of the oxygen transport orchestra found within our red blood cells. A silent symphony of symptoms may arise when iron deficiency causes its melody to fade, affecting our overall health. But have no fear—early detection combined with practical tactics can bring harmony back.

The Soft Symphony of Illnesses:

Iron deficiency frequently has a subdued tone, with its early indications easily confused with regular exhaustion or tension.

Nevertheless, the symptoms intensify as the melody goes on:

Fatigue: We feel exhausted and listless, unable to accomplish daily tasks like a city out of gasoline.

Pale Skin and Brittle Nails: As our blood's vivid color fades, our skin becomes paler and our nails become more brittle, breaking easily.

Brain Fog and Memory Losses: When our brain's iron-fueled orchestra falters, it can cause problems with concentration, memory, and mental clarity.

Breathlessness and dizziness: Our lungs work harder to make up for the decreased oxygen delivery, which leaves us feeling out of breath and disoriented.

Mood Swings and Irritability: When the emotional melody is disturbed, irritability, mood swings, and even depression are heightened.

Revealing the Iron Thief: Identification and Verification

A straightforward blood test is necessary for a conclusive diagnosis, even though symptoms can offer hints. By measuring hemoglobin levels, ferritin **(iron storage),** and other markers, this **"iron symphony analysis"** reveals the actual severity of the iron deficiency.

Writing a Reconstruction Symphony: Resolving the Iron Disproportion

With the diagnosis in hand, we can restore the iron balance using a multifaceted strategy:

Nutritional Balance: The Strength of Plant-Based Iron Superstars
The main players in our dietary orchestra are legumes like beans and lentils, leafy greens like kale and spinach, whole grains like quinoa and oats, and nuts and seeds like pumpkin and sesame seeds. These foods high in iron from plants give our bodies the melody they need.

Vitamin C: The Artificer of Permeation

Citrus fruits and peppers contain vitamin C, which functions as a conductor by binding to iron and promoting its absorption. Iron-rich foods work best when paired with vitamin C-rich foods to bring out the best in the melody.

Cooking Mildly: Maintaining the Iron Notes

The iron melody may be muted by harsh cooking techniques. Iron content is retained in food by steaming, simmering, and other gentle cooking methods, which keeps our food colorful and iron-rich.

Supplementing with Iron: When the Symphony Requires a Lift

In certain instances, a medical practitioner might suggest iron supplements as a concentrated form of iron that can quickly replenish optimal levels and enhance the tone.

Beyond the Plate: Improving Absorption of Iron and Treating Fundamental Causes

Recall that everybody is different and that certain things can impact how well iron is absorbed.

Speak with a medical expert for specific advice on:

Underlying Medical Conditions: Iron absorption may be hampered by a number of medical conditions. Maintaining long-term iron balance requires addressing these fundamental problems.

Medication: Iron absorption may be impacted by certain medications. It's crucial to discuss any possible interactions with your doctor.

Lifestyle Factors: Sleep, stress, and exercise can all affect how well iron is absorbed. Your body can use iron more efficiently if you make these life-improving changes.

Boosting Your Plant-Based Adventure: Self-Assurance in Every Bite

You can confidently navigate your plant-based journey by being aware of the diagnosis and taking appropriate action to address iron deficiency. Recall that you are the conductor of the symphony of your health. You can make sure your body gets the iron it needs to thrive by eating a varied and iron-rich diet, using absorption-boosting techniques, and getting knowledgeable advice. Raise a fork to health that is rich in iron and turn on some music!

Bonus Tip: Because fermented plant foods like miso and tempeh naturally contain probiotics, they can improve the absorption of iron.

Accept the strength of iron, identify the imbalance clearly, and create a harmonious composition of health in each mouthful!

Chapter 2:

Developing a Plant-Based Iron Powerhouse Diet: Provide Your Body with Tasty Plenty

Adopting a plant-based diet shouldn't mean sacrificing iron, which is the orchestra conductor of your body's oxygen. Although meat has easily absorbed heme iron, the kingdom of plants has a rich and varied repertoire of iron-rich treasures that are just waiting to be discovered. Together, we can create a plant-based iron powerhouse diet that will fuel your body and ignite your health with every bite of food.

The Lead Singers: Iron-Rich Powerhouses from Plants

Legumes such as lentils and beans, chickpeas and black beans, nature's powerhouses full of non-heme iron, are the first in your plant-based iron orchestra. The vibrant harmonies added by leafy greens such as kale, spinach, arugula, and collard greens amplify the iron melody. Whole grains add their own iron-rich notes to the chorus, such as quinoa, oats, brown rice, and millet. Remember the percussion section as well. Nuts and seeds such as almonds, sunflower, and sesame seeds give the dish a pleasant crunch and a surprising amount of iron.

Vitamin C and Enhancers for Absorption: The Conductor's Baton

But iron is insufficient on its own. Vitamin C is a colorful conductor that binds to non-heme iron and changes its form so that your body can absorb it easily. Broccoli, bell peppers, and citrus fruits like oranges and grapefruits serve as the conductor's indispensable baton, ensuring that the iron melody is fully realized. The color-loving conductor of leafy greens and carrots, beta-carotene, steps in to improve iron bioavailability and make sure the message reaches every cell in your body. Turmeric, an aromatic spice, contributes its own harmony and may help reduce inflammation, which can hinder the absorption of iron.

Writing the Symphony: Ingenious Food Combinations and Tasty Techniques

Creating a plant-based iron powerhouse diet is akin to creating a masterpiece in the kitchen. Use your imagination! Lentil stews become iron-absorption duets when paired with chopped tomatoes and bell peppers. Toss your quinoa salad with chopped red pepper and citrus zest to create colorful harmony. To add a chorus of iron and anti-inflammatory goodness to your leafy greens, drizzle them with a dressing infused with turmeric. Recall that diversity is essential! Taste different combinations, play around with flavors, and let your creativity run wild when it comes to cooking.

Beyond the Plate: Enhancing Assimilation and Meeting Personal Needs

Cooking techniques are important. Iron content can be preserved by soft steaming or simmering, but hard boiling can mute its flavor. Herbal teas high in iron can help your body feel better, but keep in mind that tannins in coffee and black tea can prevent your body from absorbing iron. If you require additional support, such as iron supplements, or if you have any underlying conditions that could affect your body's ability to absorb iron, speak with your healthcare provider for tailored advice.

Boosting Your Plant-Based Adventure: Self-Assurance in Every Bite

There's more to creating a plant-based iron-powerhouse diet than just eating right. It's about adopting a way of life that supports and strengthens your health. You can confidently conduct the symphony of your well-being by knowing the basics of iron absorption, experimenting with a variety of delicious foods, and seeking informed guidance when necessary. Recall that you are in charge of creating, directing, and designing your own health. Raise a fork to abundant iron-rich food and allow plant-based power to fill your plate and your life!

Bonus Tip: Because fermented plant foods like miso and tempeh naturally contain probiotics, they can improve the absorption of iron.

Accept the potential of plant-based iron, use knowledge and creativity to create a powerful diet, and then listen to the harmonious sound of your health!

○ Selecting Iron-Rich Plant Foods: A Tasty Manual for Nourishing Your Body

You shouldn't have to give up iron, the vital conductor of your internal oxygen orchestra, in order to adopt a plant-based diet. Although meat has easily absorbed heme iron, the kingdom of plants has a rich and varied repertoire of iron-rich treasures that are just waiting to be discovered. Together, we will take you on a delightful journey to select plant-based foods high in iron, enabling you to create a diet that will ignite your health and fuel your body with every meal.

Iron Powerhouses in the Plant Kingdom: The Lead Singers

The lead singers in your plant-based iron orchestra are the performers who are most powerful and possess non-heme iron. Chickpeas, black beans, lentils, and other legumes take center stage because of their high iron content, which can rival that of some meat sources. With even more iron than certain fruits, leafy greens such as kale, spinach, arugula, and collard greens contribute their colorful harmonies. Whole grains join the chorus, adding their own noteworthy iron notes—quinoa, oats, brown rice, and millet. Remember the percussion section as well. Nuts and seeds such as almonds, sunflower, and sesame seeds give the dish a pleasant crunch and a surprising amount of iron.

Beyond the Soloists: Examining Iron-Rich Foods' Supporting Ensemble

The lead singers are just one part of the iron symphony, though.

Numerous other foods made from plants contribute their own notes to the melody:

Fruits: While fresh berries like strawberries and raspberries offer a vitamin C boost to aid absorption, dried fruits like apricots, raisins, and figs are surprisingly rich in iron.

Vegetables: A variety of vegetables, such as sweet potatoes, mushrooms, and Brussels sprouts, provide differing amounts of iron, giving your iron orchestra depth and complexity.
Iron-rich foods like tofu and tempeh provide a complete protein source and a significant amount of iron.

The Conductor's Baton: Strategies for Food Pairing and Absorption Enhancers

For iron to have its full effect, a conductor is necessary, just like in any symphony. The colorful conductor, vitamin C, binds to non-heme iron to facilitate easier absorption by your body. To make sure the iron melody reaches its full potential, pair your iron-rich foods with bell peppers, broccoli, and citrus fruits like oranges and grapefruits. The master of vibrant veggies like carrots and leafy greens, beta-carotene, steps in to improve iron bioavailability while contributing its own nutritional harmony. Not to be overlooked is turmeric, an aromatic spice that may help lessen inflammation, which may hinder the absorption of iron.

Writing Your Iron-Rich Symphony: Ingenious Recipe Combinations and Tasty Suggestions

There's more to creating a plant-based iron powerhouse diet than just picking out specific foods.

It's about crafting a masterpiece of food! Here are a few delectable suggestions:

Breakfast Symphony: Begin your day with an oatmeal bowl rich in iron, garnished with berries and a squeeze of lemon juice.

Harmony over lunch: Savor a quinoa salad topped with grated red pepper flakes and zest from a citrus fruit, or a lentil stew cooked with tomatoes and bell peppers.

Savor a chickpea curry bursting with Indian spices, or a tofu stir-fry loaded with veggies and leafy greens for a dinnertime serenade.

Snacktime Interlude: Snackle on almonds and dried apricots, or savor a smoothie made with berries, spinach, and a hint of citrus.

Beyond the Plate: Enhancing Hematic Iron Absorption and Meeting Personal Needs

Recall that absorption counts. Simmering and steaming are gentle cooking techniques that maintain iron content, whereas boiling can destroy its flavor. Coffee and black tea contain tannins that can obstruct the absorption of iron. If you require additional support, such as iron supplements, or if you have any underlying conditions that could affect your body's ability to absorb iron, speak with your healthcare provider.

Boosting Your Plant-Based Adventure: Self-Assurance in Every Bite

Selecting plant-based foods high in iron is about taking responsibility for your health and wellbeing. You can confidently lead the iron-rich plant-based lifestyle symphony by using absorption enhancers, knowing the power of diversity in your food choices, and getting expert advice when necessary. Recall that you are in charge of creating, directing, and designing your own health. Now let the music of health fill your plate and your life as you raise a fork to the vibrant world of plant-based iron!

Bonus Tip: Because fermented plant foods like miso and tempeh naturally contain probiotics, they can improve the absorption of iron.

Accept the potential of plant-based iron, make informed and imaginative food choices, and listen to your body's healing orchestra!

○ Organizing Nutritious and Balanced Meals: A Tasty Symphony for Your Well-Being

Eating healthfully doesn't have to be a difficult concerto; rather, it can be a well-balanced symphony of tasty and nourishing foods. Creating a meal plan that is balanced will guarantee that your body gets the essential nutrients it needs to support overall health, energy, and mood. Let's take a culinary adventure together, learning about the essential components of well-balanced meals and creating our own masterpieces that promote health.

The Essential Nutrient Orchestra: Each food group has a vital role in the carefully constructed ensemble that is a balanced meal:

The lead singers of the macronutrient melody—carbohydrates, fats, and proteins—provide your body with energy and structural components. Select lean proteins like lentils and beans for muscle growth and repair, whole grains like quinoa and brown rice for sustained energy, and healthy fats like avocado and olive oil for satiety.

The Balance of Vitamins and Minerals: Your body's systems operate properly because of these essential micronutrients, which act as a supporting cast. For a wide variety of vitamins and minerals, such as vitamin C in citrus fruits and iron in leafy greens, include fruits and vegetables in a rainbow of colors.

The Rhythm of Fiber: Fiber, the frequently disregarded conductor of your digestive system, maintains harmony and gut health. Consume a lot of foods high in fiber, such as vegetables, legumes, and whole grains, to maintain a steady and healthy rhythm.

Writing Your Greatest Work: Useful Tips for Well-Balanced Meals

It is not necessary to have a culinary degree to prepare balanced meals; instead, try implementing these easy tips:

The Plate Model: See your plate as a canvas that is divided. Divide the contents in half; add non-starchy veggies to one quarter; add whole grains or starchy vegetables to one quarter; and top with lean protein. All dietary groups are represented in this visual guide.

Variety Is Essential: Avoid becoming mired in a food rut! To keep your meals interesting and avoid nutrient deficiencies, try experimenting with different ingredients, textures, and flavors. To keep your body and palate satisfied, experiment with different protein sources, seasonal produce, and international cuisines.

Cooking Techniques Are Important: Techniques as gentle as steaming, baking, and grilling retain nutrients and bring out flavors. Give up deep-frying and switch to healthier cooking methods that highlight the inherent goodness of your ingredients.

Considerate Portions: Recognize when your body is hungry and refrain from overindulging. To make sure you're fueling your body, not overindulging, while eating, pay attention to portion sizes and keep your eyes off of other things.

Beyond the Plate: Extra Guidance for a Healthful Way of Life

Recall that eating healthily is a lifestyle, not just a set of meals:

Water is the Conductor: It maintains the proper orchestration of your body. To stay hydrated, choose hydrating fruits and vegetables and try to drink eight glasses of water a day.

Mindful Eating: Enjoy your meal, chew it slowly, and keep your eyes off other things while you eat. This facilitates mindful eating practices and enables your body to recognize signals of fullness.

Organizing and Getting Ready: Making healthy meal and snack plans in advance can help you avoid making bad decisions when you're hungry. For easy snacking, keep wholesome staples like fruits, nuts, and pre-washed veggies close at hand.

Seek Guidance: Speak with a registered dietitian or nutritionist if you have any dietary questions or need individualized guidance. They can assist you in developing a well-balanced meal plan that suits your individual requirements and tastes.

Taking Charge of Your Health: Play Your Own Sweet Symphony

You too can be the conductor of your own health symphony by learning what makes a balanced meal, implementing doable strategies, and asking for help when necessary. Never forget that every meal counts toward your overall health story. Select a variety of ingredients, eat with awareness, and revel in the pleasure of wholesome, delectable food. Raise a fork to well-balanced meals and enjoy the soundtrack of wellbeing!

Bonus Tip: Add another level of harmony to your nutritional symphony by experimenting with fermented foods like kimchi and yogurt, which can improve gut health and nutrient absorption.

Accept the power of well-balanced meals, put creativity into your cooking, and allow health to fill your plate and your life!

○ Beyond the Hype: Revealing the Real Story of Superfoods to Increase Iron

The phrase **"superfood"** frequently evokes visions of rare fruits and pricey berries that promise to be the secret to perfect health. Iron is one of the many important nutrients that some foods are rich in, but there isn't really a one-size-fits-all approach. Together, we can break through the myths and discover the real benefits of superfoods for an iron boost, giving you the knowledge you need to make decisions that are best for your health.

Iron Symphony: Getting to Know the Players and the Conductor

Imagine your body as a busy city, with iron serving as the vital role of a conductor for the delivery of oxygen. Iron is the fuel that keeps the city's delivery vehicles, or red blood cells, operating at peak performance. While meat has easily absorbed heme iron, there are a wealth of non-heme iron treasures in the plant kingdom just waiting to be discovered.

The Lead Singers: Iron Powerhouses Made of Plants

Put away the goji and acai berries! The real iron superstars are found in the kingdom of plants; they're easily accessible and surprisingly tasty. Chickpeas, black beans, lentils, and other legumes take center stage because of their high iron content, which can rival that of some meat sources. With even more iron than certain fruits, leafy greens such as kale and spinach, arugula, and collard greens contribute their colorful harmonies. Brown rice, millet, quinoa, and oats are examples of whole grains that join the chorus and add their own noteworthy iron notes. A surprising amount of iron and a delightful crunch are added by nuts and seeds like almonds, sunflower, and sesame seeds, among others, in the percussion section. Don't forget about it.

The Conductor's Baton: Art of Pairing and Absorption Enhancers

But iron is insufficient on its own. Vitamin C is a colorful conductor that binds to non-heme iron and changes its form so that your body can absorb it easily. Broccoli, bell peppers, and citrus fruits like oranges and grapefruits serve as the conductor's indispensable baton, ensuring that the iron melody is fully realized. The master of vibrant veggies like carrots and leafy greens, beta-carotene, steps in to improve iron bioavailability while contributing its own nutritional harmony. Additionally, the fragrant spice turmeric may be able to lessen inflammation, which may hinder the absorption of iron.

Writing Your Iron Symphony: Moving Past the Hype to Practical Solutions

There's more to creating a plant-based diet high in iron than just specific ingredients. It's about creating a culinary masterpiece that fuels your body and improves your absorption, learning about different food options, and enhancing your well-being through food.

The following are some tactics:

Combine foods high in iron with foods high in vitamin C: Consider a quinoa salad topped with red pepper and citrus zest, or a lentil stew with diced tomatoes and bell peppers.

Accept the benefits of fermented foods: Iron-loving champions tempeh and miso can further improve iron absorption thanks to their natural probiotics.

Transcend the term "superfood": Prioritize eating a varied, well-balanced diet full of whole grains, fruits, vegetables, and healthy fats.

Cook with intelligence: Iron content can be preserved by soft steaming or simmering, but hard boiling can mute its flavor.

Ask for advice: If you require extra assistance or have any underlying medical conditions that impact your ability to absorb iron, speak with a registered dietitian or other healthcare provider for individualized guidance.

Taking Charge of Your Health: Managing Your Own Plate

Remind yourself that iron is not a magic fix. With knowledge of the real iron powerhouses, absorption enhancers, and knowledgeable advice, you can conduct your health like a symphony right on your plate. Let the music of well-being fill your body and your life as you embrace the delicious world of plant-based iron and throw off the hype!

Bonus Tip: Try using spices like coriander and cumin; they may improve the absorption of iron and give your food a unique taste.

Embrace a variety of nutrient-dense plant-based options and cast aside the label of **"superfood"** to experience the true symphony of iron-rich health!

○ Managing Iron Absorption: Nutritional Approaches for Ideal Consumption

Your internal oxygen orchestra's conductor, iron, is essential for energy production, brain health, and general well-being. Meat provides easily absorbed heme iron, but the kingdom of plants has a colorful array of non-heme iron treasures that are just waiting to be discovered. However, to get the most iron absorption from plant-based sources, you need to know who the main players are and how to play the melody louder.

The Maestro's Baton and Vitamin C are the Absorption Enhancers

Visualize iron as a bashful musician, straining to get attention. The bright, citrusy maestro that is vitamin C binds to non-heme iron and changes its form so that it is easily absorbed by your digestive system. Imagine it as transforming the iron into a tasty, palatable tune. Broccoli, bell peppers, and citrus fruits like oranges and grapefruits are all members of this vital chorus, prepared to add intensity to the iron symphony.

The Ensemble: The Harmonious Combination of Turmeric and Beta-Carotene

The mastermind behind vibrant veggies like carrots and leafy greens, beta-carotene, steps in to help convert non-heme iron into a form that is easier to absorb. Like a proficient technician, it adjusts the iron molecule to ensure maximum absorption. The aromatic spice turmeric adds a unique harmony and may help reduce inflammation, which can hinder the absorption of iron. Visualize it as a calming tune that fosters an atmosphere that is conducive to the absorption of iron.

Food Pairing: Crafting a Masterpiece in the Kitchen

Creating an iron-rich plant-based diet is like creating a masterpiece in the kitchen. Maximizing iron intake requires matching foods high in iron with their absorption enhancers. When lentils are cooked with tomatoes and bell peppers, the iron and vitamin C content of the stew becomes harmonious. A quinoa salad topped with chopped red pepper and zest of citrus strikes all the right notes, with each component contributing its own harmony. Never forget that originality is essential! Try out various combinations and allow your creativity to run wild when it comes to cooking.

The Restrictors: Comprehending the Off-Key Element

Certain inhibitors have the ability to muffle the melody, while enhancers amplify the iron symphony. Whole grains, legumes, and nuts contain phytates, which have the ability to bind with iron and reduce its absorption. But these foods can also be made much less phytate-y by soaking, sprouting, and fermenting, which lets the iron melody come through. Tea and coffee, which contain tannins, can also hinder the absorption of iron, so it's best to avoid having them right before or right after meals high in iron.

Enhancing Iron Symphony: Going Beyond the Plate

Your body is an important part of the iron absorption orchestra. Simmering and steaming are gentler cooking techniques that do not damage the iron molecule as much as boiling does. Iron absorption may also be impacted by specific drugs and medical conditions, so it's crucial to get advice from a healthcare provider.

Boosting Your Plant-Based Adventure: Self-Assurance in Every Bite

Knowing what promotes and hinders iron absorption will help you embrace a plant-based diet high in this essential mineral. Examine a variety of food options, try out inventive combinations, and get knowledgeable advice to create your own harmonious blend of health and wellness. Recall that your health is a conductor!

Bonus Tip: Because fermented plant foods like miso and tempeh naturally contain probiotics, they can improve the absorption of iron.

Let the celebration of iron-rich health accompany your plant-based journey. Uncover the covert thief of low iron, protect your health, and allow iron to fill your life with music!

Recall that the best possible absorption of iron is the result of a balanced combination of nutrient-dense foods, supplements that improve absorption, and conscientious eating habits. With confidence, lead your own iron symphony and relish the lively tune of well-being in every mouthful!

Part 2:

Revealing the Iron Treasures: An Adventure through the Bounty of the Plant Kingdom

Iron, the conductor of your own internal oxygen orchestra, nourishes your body, improves mental clarity, and keeps it in a state of vibrant health. Meat provides easily absorbed heme iron, but the kingdom of plants has a rich and varied repertoire of non-heme iron treasures just waiting to be unlocked. Together, let's set out on an exciting journey to uncover the gems containing iron that are hidden within nature's abundant storehouse.

The Lead Singers: Iron Powerhouses Found in Nature

Enter the lush stage, where the iron orchestra's lead singers take the spotlight. Legumes, such as black beans, chickpeas, and lentils, sing a powerful song and have iron contents that are comparable to some meat sources. Compared to certain fruits, leafy greens such as kale, spinach, arugula, and collard greens pack an even bigger iron punch with their colorful harmonies. Whole grains join the chorus with their own substantial iron notes, such as quinoa, oats, brown rice, and millet. Remember to include the percussion section as well. Nuts and seeds such as almonds, sunflower, and sesame seeds, as well as pumpkin seeds, give the dish a delightful crunch and a surprising amount of iron.

The Conductor's Baton: Using Absorption Helpers to Amplify the Iron Symphony

However, the iron melody cannot shine without a conductor. The colorful conductor, vitamin C, binds to non-heme iron and changes its form so that your body can easily absorb it. Broccoli, bell peppers, oranges, and grapefruits are examples of citrus fruits that serve as the conductor's indispensable baton, helping the iron melody to reach its full potential. The master of vibrant veggies like carrots and leafy greens, beta-carotene, steps in to improve iron bioavailability while contributing its own nutritional harmony. Additionally, the aromatic spice turmeric may lessen inflammation, which may obstruct the absorption of iron and set the stage for the iron melody to freely resonate.

Writing Your Iron-Rich Masterwork: Inventive Food Combinations and Tasty Techniques

Creating a plant-based, iron-rich diet is similar to creating a culinary masterpiece. Match your iron-dense lead singers with their absorption-enhancing partners, such as a quinoa salad dressed with chopped red pepper and citrus zest, a lentil stew simmered with tomatoes and bell peppers, or a breakfast smoothie made with spinach, berries, and a hint of citrus. Discover a variety of taste combinations and textures, such as Thai stir-fries packed with nuts and leafy greens and Indian curries full of vegetables and spices high in iron. Never forget that originality is essential! Try new things, have fun, and let your creativity run wild when it comes to cooking.

Beyond the Plate: Achieving Individual Needs and Iron Absorption Optimization

Never forget that your body is the stage, and it matters how it plays with the iron symphony. Simmering and steaming are gentle cooking techniques that maintain iron content, whereas boiling at a high temperature can mute it. Coffee and black tea contain tannins that can obstruct the absorption of iron. If you require additional support, such as iron supplements, or have any underlying conditions that affect your ability to absorb iron, speak with a healthcare provider.

Boosting Your Plant-Based Adventure: Self-Assurance in Every Bite

Discovering the iron-rich plant kingdom is about enhancing your health and wellbeing, not just about what to eat. You can conduct the iron symphony of your plant-based lifestyle with confidence if you know who the major players are, use absorption enhancers, and get knowledgeable advice when necessary. Accept the rich and varied world of iron-rich plant foods, unleash the creativity in your kitchen, and allow your plate and your life to be filled with the melodies of health!

Bonus Tip: Add some more harmony to your iron orchestra by trying fermented plant-based foods like miso and tempeh, which naturally contain probiotics that can improve iron absorption.

So let's start your journey through the kingdom of plants, rich in iron! Find the hidden gems, create your own culinary masterpiece, and savor each bite for its lively melody of health. Recall that you are in charge of your own wellbeing. Take command, accept the benefits of iron derived from plants, and allow health to radiate!

Chapter 3:

Unlocking a Nutritious Symphony on Your Plate with the Power of Legumes

The humble heroes of the plant kingdom, legumes are hiding a nutritional powerhouse symphony just waiting to be unlocked. Beneath their modest exterior, they are champions of a sustainable and healthful diet because they are a powerful source of protein, fiber, vitamins, and minerals. Let's explore the rich and varied benefits of legumes and how they can enhance your overall health as we take a closer look at them.

The Protein Powerhouse: Discard the idea that diets based solely on plants are low in protein. Nature's protein superfoods are legumes, which include beans, lentils, chickpeas, and peas. They provide complete protein profiles that include all of the essential amino acids. With a whopping 18 grams of protein in just one cup of cooked lentils, cooked lentils out protein many animal sources. This plant-based protein increases muscle growth and repair, prolongs feelings of fullness, and boosts energy levels all around.

The Conductor of Gut Health: Not only are legumes a rich source of protein, but they are also maestros of fiber. Their pair of soluble and insoluble fibers maintains regularity, supports healthy gut flora, and keeps your digestive system functioning efficiently. This symphony of fiber lowers cholesterol, helps control blood sugar, and may even offer protection against some types of cancer.

The Vitamin and Mineral Chorus: It's not all about legumes. They explode with a colorful chorus of essential vitamins and minerals, enhancing your diet and assisting with a host of body processes. Lentils and black beans are rich in iron, which is the conductor of your internal oxygen orchestra. Kidney beans and chickpeas are excellent sources of folate, which is essential for cell growth and development. Joining the chorus, magnesium, potassium, and phosphorus support nerve transmission, muscle contraction, and healthy bones.

The Sustainable Symphony: Legumes are champions of sustainability in addition to being highly nutritious foods. In comparison to animal agriculture, they use less water and land, fix nitrogen in the soil, and increase biodiversity. Legumes are a vote in favor of a more sustainable future for all people and a healthier planet.

Writing Your Chef's Masterpiece: Not only are legumes healthy, but they're also very adaptable! Their culinary repertoire is endless, ranging from creamy dips and falafels to hearty stews and soups.

Here are a few ideas for utilizing their power on your plate:

Incorporate chickpeas or lentils into your morning smoothie to add extra protein and kickstart your day.

Try a lentil salad for a tasty and nutritious lunch. Simply combine cooked lentils with chopped vegetables, fresh herbs, and a zesty vinaigrette.

Enjoy a hearty soup to warm you up: Cook a thick lentil or bean soup for a filling and healthy dinner.

Dive into yumminess: Make a black bean dip or creamy hummus with blended chickpeas for a nutritious snack or starter.

Accept the revolution in burgers and try plant-based meat substitutes like lentil, black bean, or chickpea burgers.

Beyond the Plate: Complete Living with Legumes

Legumes have power that goes beyond the plate. Legumes become more nutrient-dense and easier to digest when they sprout, and they also release more probiotics and B vitamins when they ferment. Try a variety of preparation techniques to see what works best for you.

Taking Charge of Your Health: The Navigator of Your Happiness

You take control of your own health by realizing the benefits of legumes and including them in your diet. Accept their varied nutritional symphony, discover their culinary possibilities, and rejoice in their long-term advantages. Recall that legumes are a gateway to a happier, healthier, and more sustainable you rather than just a food source.

Bonus Tip: To add even more excitement to your culinary adventure, try out heirloom bean varieties for their distinct flavors and textures.

So, allow legumes to do their magic on your plate! Discover their varied tastes, unleash their nutritional symphony, and feel the transformational power of plant-based heroes. Recall that every meal you take contributes to a symphony of health and wellbeing that permeates every area of your life, in addition to providing nourishment for your body.

○ **Iron-Driven Symphony: Revealing the Potential of Peas, Beans, and Lentils**

Beans, lentils, and peas are nature's secret orchestra of iron-rich goodness, waiting to energize your body and ignite your well-being. Don't let their modest appearance deceive you. Beneath their humble exterior, there's a symphony of essential nutrients just waiting to be unleashed in your recipes. So grab a fork and come along for an exciting exploration of these powerhouses made of iron!

The Iron Conductors: Discard the idea that diets high in plants are deficient in iron. The main actors in this iron opera are beans, lentils, and peas; their impressive iron content even matches that of some meat sources. Cooked lentils contain an impressive 18 mg of iron per cup, and black beans and chickpeas contribute significant amounts of iron as well. This easily absorbed form of non-heme iron is essential for the efficient distribution of oxygen throughout your body, which helps you stay alert and focused all day.

The Protein Harmony: However, there are other instruments in this orchestra besides iron. Peas, beans, and lentils provide a complete protein profile, which means they have every essential amino acid your body requires to function. This symphony of plant-based proteins supports muscle growth and repair, increases feelings of fullness, and powers your body's metabolism. Give up on the myths about protein and tap into the strength of these nutrient-dense superfoods!

The Fiber Chorus: This symphony's fiber section is just as remarkable. The maestros of gut health, soluble and insoluble fiber, collaborate to maintain the efficiency of your digestive system. This chorus of fiber lowers cholesterol, controls blood sugar, and fosters a healthy gut microbiome, which is the cornerstone of overall health. With each bite of these wonders rich in fiber, bid adieu to sluggishness and hello to a happy gut!

Legumes, beans, and peas are not one-trick pony crops when it comes to vitamins and minerals. They are overflowing with a varied chorus of vital vitamins and minerals, each adding a distinct melody to the overall harmony of your health. Kidney beans and chickpeas are rich in folate, the maestro of cell growth and development. Joining the chorus to support bone health, muscle function, and nerve transmission are magnesium, potassium, and phosphorus. Your body will have all the resources it needs to function at its peak thanks to this vitamin and mineral blend.

Writing Your Chef's Masterpiece: These treasures powered by iron are beautiful because of their versatility. They can be turned into culinary masterpieces, from rich stews and soups to creamy dips and burgers. To unleash their power on your plate, try these methods:

Try a lentil salad for a tasty and wholesome lunch. Simply combine cooked lentils with chopped vegetables, fresh herbs, and a zesty vinaigrette.

Warm up with a filling soup: For a cozy, high-iron dinner, simmer a potent minestrone or black bean soup.

Dive into yumminess: Make a black bean dip or blend chickpeas into hummus for a filling and healthful snack or appetizer.

Accept the revolution in burgers: Try some plant-based burgers instead of meat, like lentil, black bean, or chickpea burgers.

Take on the day with a boost of protein: Smoothie in cooked beans or lentils for a filling and stimulating breakfast.

Going Beyond the Plate: Realizing Your Complete Potential

Peas, lentils, and beans have power that goes beyond the plate. Legumes that have been sprouted have more nutrients and are easier to digest. Fermentation adds more probiotics and B vitamins to the mix, enhancing the overall health benefits. Try out various methods of preparation to see what they can accomplish!

Taking Charge of Your Health: The Navigator of Your Happiness

You take charge of your own health by realizing the iron-rich benefits of beans, lentils, and peas and incorporating them into your diet. Accept their varied nutritional symphony, discover their culinary possibilities, and rejoice in their long-term advantages. Recall that these iron-fueled gems are more than just sustenance;

they're a doorway to a more vibrant, happier, and healthier version of yourself.

So let your plate be a canvas for the iron-powered symphony of beans, lentils, and peas! Discover the nutritional value, enjoy the variety of flavors, and witness the transformational power of these plant-based superheroes. Recall that every meal you take contributes to a symphony of health and wellbeing that permeates every area of your life, in addition to providing nourishment for your body.

Bonus Tip: To add even more excitement to your culinary adventure, try out heirloom bean varieties for their distinct flavors and textures.

Accept the iron orchestra's power! Let the music of health fill your plate and your life as you unleash the symphony of beans, lentils, and peas!

○ Sprouts: The Little Iron Power Titans of Nature

Sprouts are more than just adorable salad toppings—they're those humble shoots bursting with seeds. They are the little iron giants of nature, delivering a potent dose of this necessary mineral in a small, easily absorbed capsule. As we explore the iron potential of sprouts and the surprising ways in which they can improve your health, get ready to be amazed.

Iron Symphony Amplified: Sprouts provide a vibrant melody of non-heme iron, so forget about the heavy metal of conventional iron sources. Sprouting greatly raises the bioavailability of iron in seeds, which makes it easier for your body to use even though it is not as easily absorbed as heme iron. Envision minuscule iron conductors orchestrating an array of nutrients, guaranteeing your body gets the iron it yearns for.

Powerhouse of Nutrients: This nutritional orchestra consists of more instruments than just iron. Full of vitamins, minerals, and antioxidants, sprouts are ready to balance your health. The master of iron absorption, vitamin C, joins the chorus by binding to iron and making it easier for it to enter your bloodstream. Enzymes and probiotics help with digestion and gut health, while folate, which is essential for cell growth and development, shows off its qualities. Each bite is a healthful symphony that is just waiting to be heard.

Digestive Delights: Not only are sprouts high in iron, but they are also powerful digestive agents. Proteins and complex carbohydrates are broken down into simpler forms during the sprouting process, which facilitates easier absorption by the body. This mild pre-digestion supports regularity, reduces stress on the digestive system, and feeds your gut microbiome—the basis of your general health. Think of a mild conductor that easily moves nutrients through your digestive tract.

Culinary Canvas: Sprouts are culinary chameleons as well as nutritional powerhouses. Their versatility is endless, ranging from blending into smoothies and soups to adding a vibrant crunch to salads and sandwiches. Discover the world of sprouts: add distinct textures and flavors to your food preparation with lentil, alfalfa, mung bean, and other sprouts. Never forget that originality is essential!

Sprouted Strategies: It's easy to harness the iron power of sprouts. After soaking your chosen seeds in fresh water for the entire night, give them plenty of light and ventilation. You'll have a colorful crop of little nutritional powerhouses in just two to three days, ready to eat. Try out a variety of sprouting techniques and seed types to find your favorites.

Taking Charge of Your Health: You take charge of your own health when you include sprouts in your diet. Accept their symphony of iron, discover their culinary possibilities, and rejoice in their health-giving qualities. Recall that sprouts are more than just food—they're a doorway to a more vibrant, healthy version of yourself.

Bonus Tip: Adding a layer of harmony to your health symphony, fermenting sprouts increases their nutrient content and probiotic benefits.

So, embrace the might of these little iron titans! Explore the many tastes and textures of sprouts, and feel the life-changing potential of this modest but mighty nutritional powerhouse. Keep in mind that every bite you take is contributing to a symphony of health that permeates every part of your life, not just the nourishment of your body.

Start the sprout revolution now!

○ Uncovering the Iron Powerhouse That Is Soybeans Inside

Bovine tofu, get over it! Give a standing ovation to soybeans—the humble beans with the secret iron treasure chest. They are a potent ally in your plant-based diet because, in addition to their culinary versatility, they contain a surprising amount of non-heme iron. So let's take a closer look at this nutrient-dense marvel and discover how soybeans can compose a harmonious array of health benefits for your plate.

Iron Symphony Amplified: Soybeans provide a distinct melody of non-heme iron, containing approximately 8 mg per cup of cooked beans, despite not being as easily absorbed as heme iron. This iron's special mix of ferritin and other iron-binding proteins means that, despite not being as showy as its heme counterpart, it is still functional. The conductor of iron absorption, ferritin, aids in directing iron into your bloodstream and makes sure it gets there effectively.

Nutrient Chorus: This orchestra of soybeans is made up of instruments besides iron. A colorful chorus of vitamins and minerals joins the orchestra, each one enhancing your health. Soybeans are a brilliant source of vitamin C, the maestro of iron absorption, ready to bind with iron and amplify its melody. The conductor of gut health, fiber, maintains the efficiency of your digestive system. Essential amino acids are provided by protein, the maestro of muscle building, for growth and repair. A nutritional masterpiece is waiting to be enjoyed in every bite.

Culinary Canvas: Soybeans are like chameleons in the kitchen, changing from simple beans to a wide variety of delectable options. Tofu, the unfinished product of plant-based proteins, takes in flavors like a sponge and can be added to soups, stir-fries, and even desserts. The fermented champion, tempeh, has a chewy texture and an umami-rich flavor profile that make it ideal for baking, grilling, and crumbling. The snacking superstar edamame provides a burst of protein and fiber, perfect for game nights and lunchboxes. Beyond just food, soybeans offer a gastronomic journey just waiting to be discovered.

Going Beyond the Bean: Realizing Your Complete Potential

Soybeans have more benefits than just the bean itself. In addition to being high in iron, soymilk, a dairy-free substitute, also offers a boost of calcium and vitamin D. The fermented master of umami, miso paste, enhances the flavor of soups and marinades and provides extra probiotic advantages. A textural treat, fermented tofu has even more iron and is more easily digested than regular tofu. Discover the hidden nutritional gems found in the diverse world of soy products.

Taking Charge of Your Health: The Navigator of Your Happiness

When you add soybeans to your diet, you take charge of your own health and well-being. Accept their iron-rich tune, discover their gastronomic possibilities, and rejoice in their assortment of health advantages. Keep in mind that soybeans are more than just food—they're a doorway to a more sustainable, healthy you.

Bonus Tip: Before eating, soak and sprout the soybeans to increase their nutritional content and improve digestibility, so you can enjoy their whole delicious symphony.

Raise a fork to soybeans, the iron-rich, versatile powerhouses! Taste their variety of flavors, explore their culinary potential, and witness the transformational power of this plant-based champion. Keep in mind that every bite you take is contributing to a symphony of health that permeates every part of your life, not just the nourishment of your body.

Start the revolution with soybeans!

Chapter 4:

Leafy Greens: Uncovering Nature's Iron Treasure Trove

Give way, spinach! Every leaf is a hidden jewel just waiting to be found in the colorful jungle of iron-rich wonders that is the world of leafy greens. Get rid of the boring stereotypes; these lush powerhouses provide a symphony of flavor, texture, and nutrition that will invigorate your body and improve your health. So grab a fork and come explore with us the iron treasure trove that is leafy greens!

Iron Symphony Amplified: Their delicate appearance does not deceive you. With their impressive non-heme iron content, leafy greens are nature's iron champions, even surpassing the iron content of some meat sources. A cup of cooked kale has an incredible 6 mg of iron, and collard greens and spinach add their own significant iron notes to the chorus. The melody doesn't stop there, though. These greens are a brilliant source of vitamin C, the master of iron absorption, which binds to iron and speeds up its passage into your bloodstream. It's a beautiful duet that makes sure your body gets the iron it needs.

Nutrient Orchestra: This leafy orchestra consists of more than just iron. A varied chorus of minerals and vitamins joins the symphony, each adding its own special melody to your overall health. Folate is abundant in spinach and arugula and is essential for cell growth and development. Joining the chorus is potassium, the conductor of nerve impulses, while calcium and magnesium promote healthy bones and muscles. A nutritional masterpiece is waiting to be enjoyed in every bite.

Digestive Delights: Leafy greens are a dynamo for the digestive system in addition to being high in iron. Because they are full of fiber, which is the gentle conductor of gut health, your digestive system will function more smoothly and regularly. The foundation of your overall health, your gut microbiome, is also fed by this fiber. Picture a light wind easily moving nutrients through your digestive tract.

Culinary Canvas: Leafy greens are like culinary chameleons, changing from being just plain leaves to a dazzling variety of mouthwatering options. Leafy greens thrive in salads, where they complement other vibrant veggies and sources of protein. Smoothies, the contemporary masters of the greens, combine spinach and kale to create nutrient-dense drinks that are ideal for a rapid energy boost. Leafy greens find comfort in soups and stews, which simmer them into hearty dishes that feed the body and the soul. Never forget that originality is essential!

Past the Leaf: Realizing Your Complete Potential

Leafy greens have benefits that go beyond just the crisp leaf. Sauerkraut and kimchi can be fermented to release more probiotic benefits and improve the health of your gut. Greens that have been dried concentrate their nutrients and become tasty powders that can be added to meals or blended into smoothies. Discover the hidden nutritional gems found in the diverse world of leafy green products.

Taking Charge of Your Health: The Navigator of Your Happiness

By including leafy greens in your diet, you take charge of your own health and wellness. Accept their iron-rich melody, discover their gastronomic possibilities, and rejoice in their many advantages. Recall that leafy greens are a doorway to a healthier, more vibrant you; they're more than just food.

Bonus Tip: Try out various cooking techniques. Blanching and rapid stir-frying can intensify the color of your food even more, and steaming and light sautéing retain iron content and improve flavor.

Raise a fork to leafy greens, the iron-rich plant kingdom champions! Taste their variety of flavors, explore their culinary potential, and witness the transformational power of these lush marvels. Keep in mind that every bite you take is contributing to a symphony of health that permeates every part of your life, not just the nourishment of your body.

Start the revolution with leafy greens!

○ **Beyond Spinach and Kale: Uncovering the Iron Clavier of Leafy Greens**

The poster children of the iron-rich leafy green world, kale and spinach, are deserving of a standing ovation. However, the lush platform of iron powerhouses goes well beyond these well-known individuals. Join us as we go on an exciting journey through the variety of leafy greens, each one a special instrument in a symphony of iron-rich goodness that is ready to boost your vitality and improve your health.

Boosting the Iron Symphony: Their fragile appearance does not deceive. The high non-heme iron content of leafy greens frequently equals that of some meat sources. A modest cup of cooked collard greens contains an incredible 8 mg of iron, and Swiss chard and arugula add their own powerful iron notes to the chorus. The melody doesn't stop there, though. Many green foods are rich in vitamin C, the master of iron absorption, which binds to iron and makes it easier for it to enter your bloodstream. Envision a melodic duet that makes sure your body gets the essential iron it needs.

The Nutrient Orchestra: This leafy orchestra consists of more than just iron. A varied chorus of minerals and vitamins joins the symphony, each adding its own special melody to your overall health. Watercress and mustard greens are rich sources of folate, which is essential for cell growth and development. Joining the chorus is potassium, the conductor of nerve impulses, while calcium and magnesium promote healthy bones and muscles. A nutritional masterpiece is waiting to be enjoyed in every bite.

Digestive Delights: Leafy greens are a dynamo for the digestive system in addition to being high in iron. Because they are full of fiber, which is the gentle conductor of gut health, your digestive system will function more smoothly and regularly. The foundation of your overall health, your gut microbiome, is also fed by this fiber. Picture a light wind easily moving nutrients through your digestive tract.

Beyond Spinach and Kale: Revealing Hidden Treasures

Although spinach and kale are well-known, there are numerous other hidden jewels in the iron treasure trove of leafy greens:

Microgreens: Packed with concentrated nutrients, these little powerhouses can provide up to four times the iron content of mature greens. For an iron boost, sprinkle some on sandwiches, salads, or smoothies.

Bok choy: This adaptable green, often used in stir-fries, has a mild, slightly peppery flavor and a high iron content. Try a variety of cooking techniques to realize its full potential.

Dandelion greens: Don't be duped by their sour reputation! Dandelion greens have a distinct earthy flavor and are surprisingly high in iron. For a taste of the wild, blend them into smoothies or add them to salads.

Romaine lettuce: This adaptable green is used for more than just Caesar dressings. Romaine is a great addition to wraps, burgers, and stir-fries because of its high iron content and satisfying crunch.

Chef's Canvas: Leafy greens are culinary chameleons that can change from being plain leaves to a vibrant rainbow of mouthwatering possibilities. Leafy greens thrive in salads, where they complement other vibrant veggies and sources of protein. Smoothies, the contemporary masters of the greens, combine spinach and kale to create nutrient-dense drinks that are ideal for a rapid energy boost. Leafy greens find comfort in soups and stews, which simmer them into hearty dishes that feed the body and the soul. Never forget that originality is essential!

Past the Leaf: Realizing Your Complete Potential

Leafy greens have benefits that go beyond just the crisp leaf. Sauerkraut and kimchi can be fermented to release more probiotic benefits and improve the health of your gut. Greens that have been dried concentrate their nutrients and become tasty powders that can be added to meals or blended into smoothies. Discover the hidden nutritional gems found in the diverse world of leafy green products.

Taking Charge of Your Health: The Navigator of Your Happiness

A diet rich in leafy greens can lead to a state of well-being where you are the conductor of your own health symphony. Accept their iron-rich melody, discover their gastronomic possibilities, and rejoice in their many advantages. Recall that leafy greens are a doorway to a healthier, more vibrant you; they're more than just food.

Bonus Tip: Try out various cooking techniques. Blanching and rapid stir-frying can intensify the color of your food even more, and steaming and light sautéing retain iron content and improve flavor.

Raise a fork, then, to the colorful world of leafy greens—the unsung heroes of the plant kingdom! Taste their distinct flavors, explore their culinary potential, and witness the transformational power of these lush marvels. Keep in mind that every bite you take is contributing to a symphony of health that permeates every part of your life, not just the nourishment of your body.

Let leafy greens begin their symphony of iron!

○ Leafy Greens: Using the Correct Cooking Techniques Can Take Them From Humble to Heavenly

Leafy greens, nature's emerald jewels, provide a plethora of health benefits, from vibrant vitamins and gut-loving fiber to iron-rich energy. However, their delicate nature can be intimidating, leading to soggy, wilted mess frequently. Warriors of green, do not fear! These leafy friends can be turned into flavorful, nutrient-dense culinary masterpieces with a few easy techniques.

Accept the Quick Cook: Vibrant greens are harmed by overcooking. Their texture, color, and valuable nutrients are stolen by high heat and lengthy cooking times.

Try to use gentle techniques:

Steaming: This gentle technique brightens colors and retains nutrients. Put some water in a steamer basket, bring it to a boil, and steam the greens for just two to three minutes, or until they are crisp-tender.

Blanching: The greens are shocked by a brief immersion in boiling water and then placed in an ice bath, which halts the cooking process and preserves color. Ideal for stir fries and salads.

Sautéing: Stir-fry greens for one to two minutes over medium heat with very little oil to preserve their crispness and bright colors.

Boost the Flavor Symphony: Leafy greens have a hint of bitterness, but you can bring out their earthy tones and hidden sweetness with a few easy tips:

Acidic Accents: Squeezing lime, lemon, or a little vinegar enhances flavor and facilitates the absorption of iron.

Salty Harmonies: The inherent sweetness of greens is enhanced by a dash of soy sauce or a pinch of sea salt.

Spicy Delights: To add a little heat and complexity, try adding some red pepper flakes, chili flakes, or harissa.

Aromatic Adventures: Shallots, garlic, and ginger give the flavor profile depth and warmth. Don't limit yourself to just raw leaves—mix and match textures! Try experimenting with various textures to produce tasty dishes:

Finely chopped greens blend seamlessly into soups and stews, boosting nutritional value without overpowering the dish's texture.

Shredded cheese: Denser cheese holds up better to dressings and sauces and gives salads and wraps a satisfying bite.

Rubbing: Rubbing raw kale with salt and olive oil softens the rough fibers and produces a flavorful, tender salad green.

Beyond the Fundamentals: Expand your horizons beyond the typical suspects! Try a variety of leafy greens; they all have different tastes and textures.

Spicy arugula: Gives pesto and salads a burst of pepper.
Nutmeg Swiss chard makes a tasty side dish when sautéed with garlic and lemon.

Earthy collard greens: These become a comforting dish when they are braised in broth and smoked paprika.

Baby spinach that is tender is ideal for quick wilting in omelets or stir-fries.

Extra Advice:

To get rid of any grit, thoroughly wash the greens.
To add more flavor and nutrients to sauces or soups, use the cooking liquid left over after steaming or blanching greens.

For an added flavor boost, try adding garlic, herbs, or chilies to your cooking oil.

Try both cooked and raw greens to see which texture suits you best.

Leafy greens have hidden potential that can be unlocked with these easy strategies. Take a look at a world of bright flavors and textures, grab your favorite bunch, and embrace the quick cook. Recall that preparing greens is an artistic endeavor that allows you to savor the abundance of nature with every mouthwatering bite, rather than merely focusing on nutrition.

Happy travels on the green side!

○ Leafy Greens: From Opponent to Center Stage

Leafy greens, the emerald champions of nature, are too frequently reduced to supporting roles in culinary endeavors. However, what if I told you that these colorful powerhouses could take center stage and turn your meals into nutrient-dense symphonies? Together, we will explore delicious ways to add greens to dishes that will both tantalize your taste buds and nourish your body. Join us on this delicious journey.

Breakfast Bonanza: Make greens the morning maestros of your plate and eschew sugary cereals. Smoothie kale and spinach together, then add mango and pineapple for a tropical touch. Prepare a delicious avocado toast and place a bed of sautéed Swiss chard with a balsamic reduction on top. Alternatively, add chopped collard greens to your scrambled eggs to give them a smoky, bacon-like flavor for a savory twist.

Lunchtime luminaries: You don't have to eat boring salads! Give up iceberg lettuce and make colorful leafy dishes instead. Combine romaine lettuce, roasted chickpeas, crumbled feta, and a zesty lemon-tahini dressing to create a Mediterranean-style bowl. Combine black beans, quinoa, mixed greens, and a hot avocado-cilantro dressing to make a power salad. Alternatively, simmer a hearty minestrone soup, letting kale, spinach, and other greens dance with hearty vegetables and beans, for a comforting hug in a bowl.

Dinnertime Delights: Leafy greens don't have to be the supporting cast; they can steal the show. Transform portobello mushrooms into succulent meat sculptures by helping them with roasted vegetables, creamy cashew sauce, and sautéed arugula. Place a colorful layer of chopped spinach inside bell peppers to add some color and nutrients after stuffing them with a quinoa and lentil mixture. For a more international take, try stir-frying crispy tofu with broccoli, bok choy, and a sweet-spicy sesame sauce. Each bite will tantalize your senses.

Past the Plate: Greens aren't limited to salads and sides.

Try out some imaginative applications:

Leafy Green Fritters: Process the greens, spices, and chickpeas into a batter; cook in the oil until golden, then serve with a dipping sauce.

Green Goddess Pesto: This creamy pesto made with blended kale, basil, nuts, and garlic is excellent on sandwiches, pasta, and soups.

Savory Green Pancakes: For a wholesome and delectable twist, mix chopped greens into the pancake batter.

Leafy Green Chips: For a crunchy, filling snack, bake or dehydrate kale leaves.

Recall:

Maintain freshness: To avoid wilting, thoroughly wash and store greens in a dry place.

Accept rapid cooking: Sautéing, steaming, and blanching help to retain texture and nutrients.

Use your imagination when selecting flavors: Try different combinations of herbs, spices, and sauces until you find what works best.

Don't be scared to combine different leafy greens to find new tastes and textures.

So let leafy greens take center stage and unleash your inner culinary maestro. You can create dishes that are not only nutritious but also flavorful and will make you swoon over these emerald champions with a little imagination and these easy pointers.

Good appetite!

Chapter 5:

Beyond the Salad Bowl: Diverse Fruits and Vegetables Provide a Rainbow of Iron Sources

Your body uses iron, which is a conductor of energy, in meat sources. But fear not, heroes of the plant world! A varied symphony of iron-rich delights can be found in Mother Nature's colorful kingdom of fruits and vegetables, ready to fill your days with flavor and energy. So, let go of the monotony of iron and take a trip through a rainbow of delicious iron!

Unleashing the Iron Symphony: Non-heme iron, the master of plant-based iron, needs a little more attention to develop to its full potential. Heme iron, which is found in meat, is easily absorbed. Here's where the colorful chorus of veggies and fruits enters the picture. They might not have the highest iron content per serving, but their special blend of fiber, vitamins, and minerals makes the ideal environment for absorbing iron, adding a powerful note to overall health.

Iron Powerhouses in Orange, Yellow, and Red: Follow the brilliant colors! Red bell peppers, in particular, are a powerful source of iron, providing 1.5 mg per cup. Tomatoes and strawberries also contribute iron, at 0.9 and 0.7 mg, respectively. These fruits are a brilliant source of vitamin C, the shining star of this iron opera that waltzes into your bloodstream by binding to iron.

Leafy greens, nature's emerald champions, are iron powerhouses hidden in plain sight. Meet the Green Giants of Iron. With a whooping 2 mg of iron per cup, kale is the king of the green scene. Collard greens and spinach contribute 1 mg each. Remember broccoli, the cruciferous champion that provides an abundance of other nutrients and 0.7 mg of iron per cup.

Secret Treasures in the Brown and Purple Chorus: Never undervalue the influence of the darker colors! With up to 2 mg of iron per cup, dried fruits such as raisins and prunes provide a concentrated dose of iron. The legume rockstars, black beans and lentils, join the group with 3 mg and 6 mg of iron per serving, respectively. Not to be overlooked is the humble potato, a versatile iron maestro that provides 1 mg per medium-sized baked potato.

Techniques for Cooking with Iron Harmony: Remember, the right conductor is necessary for a harmonious symphony. The following advice can help you get the most iron from fruits and vegetables:

Eat foods high in iron with foods high in vitamin C, such as tomatoes, bell peppers, or citrus fruits, to increase the absorption of iron.
Don't overdo the tannins: Limit your intake of tea and coffee around meals high in iron because they can hinder the absorption of iron.
Accept fermentation: Foods that have undergone fermentation, such as sauerkraut and kimchi, can increase the bioavailability of iron.

Add some spice: Include a pinch of both black pepper and turmeric in your meals that are high in iron.

Past the Plate: Realizing Your Complete Potential: Fruits and vegetables have power that goes beyond the plate. You can add iron-rich goodness to your daily routine by blending kale into smoothies, adding dried fruit to yogurt, or having roasted chickpeas as a snack. Have fun and try new things!

Taking Charge of Your Health: The Navigator of Your Welfare: Through the integration of a wide variety of fruits and vegetables high in iron into your diet, you take on the role of the conductor of your own health orchestra. Accept the colorful tune of iron, discover the culinary possibilities of these miracles from plants, and rejoice in their many health advantages. Recall that fruits and vegetables are your doorway to a healthier, more energetic version of yourself. They are not just food.

Bonus Tip: For unusual flavors and possibly higher nutrient content, look into heirloom fruit and vegetable varieties.

Raise your fork to the rainbow of plant-based iron sources, then! Experience the transformative power of these vibrant wonders, explore their culinary potential, and savor their diverse flavors. Keep in mind that every bite you take is contributing to a symphony of health that permeates every part of your life, not just the nourishment of your body.

Let the rainbow of fruits and vegetables that are rich in iron begin!

○ **Iron Past the Orchard: Revealing Undiscovered Treasures in the Fruit Kingdom**

Apples and oranges, move aside! Beyond the typical suspects, the world of iron-rich fruits offers a vibrant symphony of deliciousness and undiscovered nutritional power. Mother Nature's abundance offers a varied chorus of fruits that are ready to increase your energy and nourish your body with every bite, so forget about the monotony of iron supplements. So grab a fork and come along on a journey where treasures rich in iron wait beyond the orchard!

The Unsung Heroes: Many lesser-known fruits can produce beautiful iron melodies, but berries and citrus fruits frequently take center stage. Sun-kissed champions of the fruit kingdom, dried figs provide an impressive 5 mg of iron per cup, making them a convenient and filling snack. The tropical powerhouse guava contributes a whopping 2.4 mg of iron per cup, enhanced by a vitamin C boost for better absorption. Remember the humble date, the iron-rich warrior of the desert, which provides 1.6 mg per cup along with a wealth of fiber for gut health.

Exotic Melodies: Go beyond the recognizable and discover the world's iron-rich treasures. The fiery maestro of the desert, the prickly pear cactus, delivers 1.4 mg of iron per cup and has a distinct flavor that can be consumed raw, juiced, or even grilled. The queen of tropical fruits, jackfruit, adds to the chorus with 1 mg of iron per cup and a meaty texture that goes well with savory cooking. Passion fruit adds a burst of tropical sunshine with a flavor as vibrant as its color and 0.6 mg of iron per cup.

Iron is useful for more than just snacks and sweets: Go Beyond the Fruit Bowl! Look for inventive ways to include these fruits, which are high in iron, in your meals:

Breakfast Brilliance: For a sweetness boost and a sneaky iron punch, blend some dried figs into your morning smoothie. For a tropical treat, sprinkle granola and chopped guava over your yogurt. Alternatively, use chopped dates to give your oatmeal a chewy, iron-rich twist.

Midday Stars: Toss in some prickly pear cactus slices for a distinctive crunch and a boost of iron to your salad. Replace the rice in your burrito bowl with jackfruit for a tasty and healthy substitute. Grilled pineapple slices with a balsamic vinegar drizzle make a cool side dish that combines sweetness and savory flavors with a hint of iron.

Dinnertime Delights: Add a hint of sweetness and subliminal iron to your Moroccan tagine by adding dried figs. Incorporate passion fruit into your curry sauce to add a taste of the tropics and an iron boost. Additionally, stuff dates with a combination of nuts and herbs for a tasty and wholesome vegetarian main course.

Recall:

Variety is essential. Take more than one fruit that is high in iron. To make sure you receive the full range of nutrients, mix and match.

Your friend is vitamin C: To optimize iron absorption, combine foods high in vitamin C, such as bell peppers or citrus fruits, with fruits high in iron.

Accept entire fruits: To preserve the fiber and other important nutrients, choose whole fruits rather than juices.

Be imaginative: Try blending and matching various textures and flavors to create the ideal iron-rich concoctions.

So let go of iron monotony and welcome the colorful melody of fruits high in iron! Explore the world of exotic treasures and venture beyond the usual suspects to uncover the power and deliciousness concealed within these unsung heroes. Not only will you be feeding your body with each bite, but you will also be orchestrating a health symphony that permeates every area of your life.

Recall that the fruit kingdom is teeming with surprises rich in iron just waiting to be uncovered. Begin your journey right now!

- **Vegetables as Iron Allies: From Roots to Bulbs**

Forget the antiquated notion that vegetables are only ancillary players in the game of absorbing iron. The vegetable kingdom provides a colorful symphony of iron-rich allies, ready to fuel your body and energize your days, from modest roots to radiant bulbs. So put on your gardening gloves and come explore with us below ground, where iron treasures lie hidden!

Dive deep into the earth and uncover the iron champions hiding beneath its surface in **"Rooted in Iron."** The ruby-red warriors, beets, are a powerful source of antioxidants and nitrates, and they also boast an impressive 2 mg of iron per cup.

Be not underestimated: one medium-sized baked potato contains one milligram of iron. Try parsnips, too—creamy white root vegetables with a decent 0.6 mg of iron per cup—for a startling change of pace.

Bursting with Iron: Take a look above the ground and be amazed by the iron-rich treasures that lie beneath the surface of bulbs. The humble champions, turnips, contribute 1 mg of iron per cup, while their leafy greens contribute 2 mg of iron. The master of anise-infused fennel adds a distinctive flavor to soups and salads and provides 0.6 mg of iron per cup. Along with its anti-inflammatory qualities, ginger, the fiery bulb, contributes 0.3 mg of iron per 100g for a taste of the tropics.

Beyond the Typical Suspects: While well-known veggies like broccoli and spinach frequently take center stage, there are a lot of unsung heroes who also merit praise. Spicy and packed with iron, a medium artichoke provides 1.5 mg. Artichokes are a tasty and nourishing food. The adaptable pods known as okra join the chorus by contributing 0.7 mg of iron per cup and giving stews and stir-fries a distinct taste and texture. Sun-dried tomatoes, the concentrated iron champions, offer a taste of the Mediterranean with 8 mg per cup.

Using Bulbs and Roots to Create Culinary Delights: The earthy exterior should not deceive you.

These veggies, high in iron, can be turned into culinary masterpieces:

Roasted Symphony: For a colorful and flavorful side dish, roast potatoes, parsnips, and beets with olive oil and herbs.

Creamy Concerto: Mash turnips with potatoes to make a rich, comforting dish, or blend turnip greens into your soup to add extra nutrients.

Fennel Fantasia: To create a savory and sweet foundation for fish or poultry, sauté fennel with onions and garlic.

Ginger Harmony: To add a warming and iron-rich kick to your stir-fries, marinades, or even teas, add some ginger.

Sun-Dried Sonata: For a concentrated punch of iron and flavor, add sun-dried tomatoes to salads, pasta meals, or even pizza.

Recall:

Variety is essential. Combine various vegetables high in iron to make sure you're getting a wide variety of nutrients.

Cooking techniques are important: Iron content can be preserved by steaming, roasting, and gently sautéing; overcooking can result in losses.

Liven it up: Try experimenting with other spices such as black pepper and turmeric, as they can help improve the absorption of iron.

Accept fermentation: Sauerkraut and kimchi are examples of fermented veggies that can increase iron bioavailability.

So grab your cooking skills and set out on a tasty journey with these veggies that are high in iron! Explore the underappreciated powerhouses of the vegetable kingdom, from the sun-kissed bulbs to the depths of the earth, and enjoy the symphony of health that each bite brings. Never forget that the path to iron-rich bliss begins beneath your feet!

Start the revolution with vegetables!

- ○ **Unlocking the Iron Symphony: Methods to Increase Fruit and Vegetable Absorption**

Your body uses iron, which is a conductor of energy, in meat sources. But fear not, fans of plant-based diets! A varied orchestra of iron-rich delights awaits you in the colorful kingdom of fruits and vegetables, ready to fill your days with flavor and energy. But the rhythm of iron absorption can be a little off.

Here are some pointers to boost the beat and get the most iron possible from these wonders of plant-based nutrition:

Vitamin C: The Master of Absorption: Vitamin C is the iron absorption spotlight. Add bell peppers, tomatoes, strawberries, and citrus fruits to your meals that include fruits and vegetables high in iron. These iron-binding vitamin C superstars change iron into a form your body can absorb more readily. Think of them as excited ushers, bringing the iron to the bloodstream's main platform.

Enhance the Harmony: Certain spices, such as black pepper and turmeric, can also improve the absorption of iron. The natural chelator curcumin found in turmeric increases the solubility and absorbability of iron. Piperine from black pepper accomplishes the same thing, polishing the iron for a seamless entry into your system like a backstage helper.

Forget the Tannins and Embrace the Fermentation: Tannins are present in red wine, tea, and coffee and can bind to iron to prevent it from being absorbed. Consume these drinks in moderation, particularly before or after meals high in iron. On the other hand, fermenting foods like sauerkraut and kimchi can increase the bioavailability of iron. Iron-containing compounds are broken down by these gut-friendly champions, facilitating easier absorption by your body. Imagine them as the backstage crew, getting the iron ready for its big reveal.

Cooking Techniques Matter: The villain of iron absorption may be overcooking. When steaming, blanching, or quickly stir-frying, choose gentle cooking techniques to protect the valuable iron in your fruits and vegetables. Think of them as delicate instruments that only require a little heat to produce their melodic irony.

Soak, Sprout, and Blend: Phytic acid, which is present in some fruits and vegetables such as lentils, beans, and nuts, can prevent the body from absorbing iron. Iron can be more easily absorbed from these foods by soaking, sprouting, or fermenting them to lower the phytic acid content. By dissolving the cell walls in fruits and vegetables and increasing the iron's accessibility to your body, blending them can also improve iron absorption. Imagine them as backstage workers pulling back the curtains so the iron is visible.

The key to absorbing iron is variety: Take more than one fruit or vegetable that is high in iron. Throughout the day, combining various sources makes sure you're getting the full range of nutrients and iron forms. It's similar to leading a symphony with a variety of instruments, each bringing a distinct iron melody to the whole harmony.

Recall that optimizing iron absorption requires collaboration! You can turn fruits and vegetables from just iron-rich players into potent conductors of your health symphony by implementing these suggestions into your daily routine. Now pick up a fork, enjoy the bright tune of plant-based iron, and witness the transforming potential of these tasty and nourishing friends!

Bonus Tip: To further improve absorption, pair protein sources like eggs, tofu, or lentils with fruits and vegetables high in iron. In the absorption stage, the protein functions as a spotlight, highlighting the iron and making it stand out.

Fruits and vegetables contain an iron symphony that can be fully discovered with a little imagination and these easy pointers. So enjoy the music that is high in iron and fuels your body with each mouthwatering bite!

Chapter 6:

Grains and Cereals: A Foundation for Iron Intake

The world of grains and cereals is a vibrant canvas for iron-rich wonders – forget about the bland stereotypes! These culinary chameleons, which range from common oats to age-old superfoods, offer a symphony of flavors and textures while subtly bolstering your iron intake. So give up taking iron supplements and realize how delicious these common heroes can be!

Introducing the Iron Champions: Their modest look doesn't deceive you. Cereals and grains have high iron content, frequently equal to or higher than some meat sources. Consider quinoa, the protein-dense grain that rules the kingdom and provides an astounding 8 mg of iron per cooked cup. The gentle giants of breakfast, oats, contribute 6 mg to the chorus, while fortified cereals make a creditable 5 mg contribution. Brown rice, barley, and even teff, the miracle grain of Ethiopia, join the chorus and contribute a variety of flavors and iron-rich goodness, so the iron symphony doesn't end there.

Expanding on the Single Note: Boosting Absorption Even though grains and cereals have a high iron content, your body doesn't always absorb their flavor well. Relax, the balance of nutrients holds the key! Citrus fruits, bell peppers, and tomatoes are rich in vitamin C, the master of iron absorption. When you combine these vitamin C powerhouses with your iron-dense grains and cereals, watch the wonders of absorption happen. Think of them as excited ushers, bringing the iron to the bloodstream's main platform.

Add Flavor to the Iron Symphony. Some spices can also take center stage in the opera about iron absorption. The natural chelator curcumin found in turmeric increases the solubility and absorbability of iron. Piperine from black pepper joins the chorus, boosting iron absorption the way a backstage assistant shines the iron for a seamless transition into your system.

Phytates: Never Fear Them: Phytic acid, a naturally occurring substance found in some grains and cereals, can prevent the absorption of iron. Don't worry, though; these villains can become heroes who boost iron with a few simple techniques! Your grains and cereals can have their phytic acid content lowered and their iron content increased by soaking, sprouting, and fermenting them. Consider them as the iron's backstage technicians, getting it ready for its big reveal.

Beyond the Bowl: Unlocking the Potential of Grain Cereals and grains aren't just for breakfast!

Try experimenting with their variety in cooking:

Savory Symphony: You can use quinoa in salads, soups, and even stuffed bell peppers with a mixture of lentils and quinoa.

Oatmeal Delights: Oats can be used as a gluten-free flour substitute, blended into smoothies, or baked into muffins.

Rice Revolution: To make a filling dinner, quickly cook brown rice, veggies, and protein together.

Barley Bonanza: To add chewiness and iron to stews and soups, use barley.

Teff Twist: For a distinctive and iron-rich experience, try Ethiopian injera bread baked with teff flour.

Recall:

Variety is essential. For a variety of nutrients and forms of iron, switch up your cereals and grains throughout the day.

Cook carefully: To retain iron content, use gentle methods such as simmering or steaming.

Accept fermentation: Sourdough bread and other fermented grains can increase the bioavailability of iron.

Remember to take your vitamin C: For best absorption, combine your vitamin C-rich fruits and vegetables with your iron-rich grains.

Put your fork up to the iron-packed potential of cereals and grains! With each bite, these unsung heroes provide a scrumptious and nourishing base for your health, ready to create a harmonious wholeness. Savor their variety of tastes, investigate their culinary possibilities, and be amazed by the miracles rich in iron that these foods can do!

Bonus Tip: If you have higher iron requirements, fortified foods are an excellent way to increase your intake of the mineral. Just keep in mind that different types of iron are better absorbed than others, so be sure to read the labels.

You can unlock the full potential of the iron symphony hidden within grains and cereals with a little imagination and these easy tips. So enjoy every tasty and nourishing grain while your body is nourished by the iron-rich music!

○ Entire Grains: The Raw Iron Treasures Found in Nature

Get over the tasteless preconceptions about processed grains! The unprocessed champions of the cereal kingdom, whole grains are the jewels of nature, rich in iron, just waiting to be discovered. Not only are they nutrient-dense powerhouses, but they also play melodies in the symphony of iron absorption, ready to fill your days with flavor and energy. So embrace the unrefined revolution and throw out your iron supplements!

Iron Symphony Unadulterated: Unlike refined grains, whole grains keep their bran and germ—the iron-rich grain world's treasure troves. The protein-dense king of the whole grain kingdom, quinoa, contributes an impressive 8 mg of iron per cooked cup. Meanwhile, oats, the breakfast bards, contribute 6 mg. Rich in iron and bursting with flavor, brown rice, barley, and even the Ethiopian iron maestro, teff, all contribute their distinct voices to the symphony.

Unleashing the Absorption Melody: Although whole grains have a high iron content, your body doesn't always absorb their melody easily. But do not worry—nutrient harmony holds the key! Citrus fruits, bell peppers, and tomatoes are rich sources of vitamin C, which is a conductor of iron absorption. When these iron-rich whole grains are combined with these vitamin C superstars, the magic of absorption will happen.

Think of them as excited ushers, bringing the iron to the bloodstream's main platform.

Enhancing the Iron Symphony: Specific spices have the potential to take center stage in the opera about iron absorption. The natural chelator curcumin found in turmeric increases the solubility and absorbability of iron. Piperine from black pepper joins the chorus, boosting iron absorption the way a backstage assistant shines the iron for a seamless transition into your system.

Beyond the Cereal Bowl: Revealing the Potential of Whole Grain: Not only are whole grains great for breakfast!

They provide a wide range of gastronomic options:

Savory Serenade: For a filling and iron-rich supper, stuff bell peppers with a mixture of quinoa and lentils. You can also add quinoa to salads and soups.

Oatmeal Opera: To add more fiber and iron to your baking, you can blend oats into smoothies, bake them into muffins, or use them as a substitute for gluten-free flour.

Rice Rhapsody: To make a filling and savory dish, quickly cook brown rice, veggies, and protein together.

Barley Bonanza: To give stews and soups a chewy texture and an additional fiber and iron boost, add barley.

Teff Twist: For a distinctive and iron-rich experience, try Ethiopian injera bread baked with teff flour.

Recall:

Variety is essential. Vary your whole grain intake throughout the day to get a variety of nutrients and forms of iron.

Cook carefully: To retain the goodness of whole grains and to preserve iron content, use gentle cooking techniques like steaming or simmering.

Accept fermentation: Sourdough bread, one type of fermented whole grain, can increase the body's absorption of iron.

Remember to take your vitamin C: For best absorption, combine your vitamin C-rich fruits and vegetables with your iron-rich whole grains.

Raise a fork to the raw revolution in whole grains, then! With every bite, these iron-rich champions provide a tasty and nutritious base for your health, allowing it to blossom into a harmonious whole. Savor their variety of tastes, investigate their culinary possibilities, and be amazed by the transformational power of these raw iron gems!

Bonus Tip: To get an additional dose of iron and other nutrients, look for whole grains like spelt, kamut, and amaranth. They may end up being your new favorite iron symphony songs!

Whole grains contain an unprocessed iron symphony that can be fully realized with a little imagination and these easy pointers. So enjoy the music that is high in iron and use every tasty and nourishing bite to fuel your body!

- **Quinoa and Amaranth: Historic Grains, Contemporary Wonders**

Quinoa and amaranth are two ancient stars in the colorful kingdom of grains. Originating in the Andes and Mesoamerica, respectively, these gluten-free marvels are not historical artifacts but rather contemporary nutritional marvels with an array of health advantages and culinary adaptability. Now that you're ready to explore these ancient grains and satisfy your palate, break free from the monotony of carbs!

Superfoods: Apart from their remarkable ancestral lineage, quinoa and amaranth are nutrient-dense superfoods. They are rare among plants in that they are complete proteins, meaning they have all nine essential amino acids. In addition, they are loaded with antioxidants, fiber, vitamins, and minerals, which makes them powerful allies in lowering inflammation, improving immunity, and controlling digestion. The iron queen, amaranth, takes the title with an incredible 9 mg of iron per cooked cup, significantly exceeding your daily requirements. Quinoa, the protein prince, boasts 8 mg of iron per cup.

Beyond the Salad Bowl: These ancient grains are more than just garnish for salads!

Their culinary possibilities are infinite:

Quinoa Canvas: Quinoa works well as a canvas for both savory and sweet recipes because of its mild flavor and fluffy texture. For a hearty and filling breakfast, try stuffing bell peppers with a mixture of quinoa and lentils, baking quinoa cakes flavored with herbs and spices, or making a creamy quinoa porridge.

Alchemy of Amaranth: The earthy flavor of amaranth and its tiny, popping seeds give your meals a distinctive twist. Sprinkle it on yogurt and smoothies for a nutty crunch, bake it into gluten-free bread for a healthier option, or toss it into soups and stews for a textural treat.

Taking Care When Cooking: In the kitchen, quinoa and amaranth need a bit more attention than their more sophisticated counterparts. Toasted amaranth brings out its nutty flavor, and quinoa's bitter coating can be removed by rinsing it. Simmering and steaming are two cooking techniques that help retain their valuable nutrients and fluffy texture.

Increasing Absorption: Recall that a conductor is necessary for the iron symphony! To optimize iron absorption, combine vitamin C-rich fruits and vegetables such as citrus, bell peppers, and tomatoes with quinoa and amaranth. Black pepper and turmeric are two more spices that can help to improve this process.

Ancient Grains, Present-Day Advantages: Including quinoa and amaranth in your diet is a commitment to your overall health and wellbeing, not just a taste experiment.

These historic grains provide:

Sustainable Goodness: Quinoa and amaranth are drought-tolerant and low-maintenance plants that are good for the environment.

Gut-Friendly Delights: Their high fiber content helps support a balanced microbiome, aids in digestion, and improves gut health.

Antioxidant Symphony: These grains lower the risk of chronic diseases and fight free radical damage with an abundance of antioxidants.

Energy-Boosting Potency: Their complex carbohydrates keep you energized for your daily activities by supplying you with consistent energy throughout the day.

Raise your fork, then, to the age-old wisdom of amaranth and quinoa! These contemporary miracles provide a tasty and healthful way to enhance your meals, fuel your body, and establish a connection with the lengthy history of these ancient grains. Accept their distinct tastes and culinary possibilities, and discover the transforming force of these age-old champions!

Bonus Tip: To discover differences in texture and flavor, try quinoa and amaranth varieties. Red amaranth gives your meals a burst of color and a slightly sweeter flavor, while black quinoa gives your meals a dramatic touch.

You can discover the contemporary wonders these ancient grains contain and realize their full potential with a little imagination and these easy pointers. Start the amaranth and quinoa symphony!

○ **Iron-Rich Cereals: A Handy Friend in Your Iron Race**

Sustaining optimal iron levels can seem like an overwhelming task amidst the daily chaos. But fear not, my fellow warriors of iron! Cereals with added iron are a tasty and easy way to increase your intake, which will enhance the taste and smoothness of your nutritional journey. Let us explore the realm of these contemporary superheroes, examining their advantages, possible drawbacks, and advice on maximizing their potential!

A Bowl Full of Nutritious Power: Cereals with added iron are more than just a simple breakfast option. They are frequently enhanced with B vitamins, folic acid, and whole grains, and can be an excellent source of important vitamins, minerals, and fiber. This makes them a valuable nutritional ally, particularly for growing children, expectant mothers, and athletes who have higher iron requirements. Think of them as a group of amiable superheroes, each with a special ability to promote your well-being!

Convenience Is Everything: Life gets busy, let's face it. Cereals with added iron are a convenient and quick way to get iron into your diet, even when you're on the go. They are quick and easy to make—just a bowl of milk—so they're perfect for busy mornings or busy evenings. Consider them your dependable companion, constantly prepared to offer assistance **(or more accurately, a helping hand)** when you most need it.

Beyond the Breakfast Bowl: These iron champions deserve more than just breakfast! Use your imagination to discover their adaptability. Crush them and add a crunchy, nutrient-rich garnish to fruit salad or yogurt. Use them as the foundation for homemade energy bars or blend them into smoothies for a quick breakfast. Recall that their ability to increase iron levels is not limited to the conventional breakfast environment!

Getting Through the Fortification Maze: Although iron-fortification provides a handy boost, it's crucial to pay attention to the kind of iron used. Certain cereals contain heme iron, which the body can absorb easily, while other cereals contain non-heme iron, which needs vitamin C to be absorbed as well as possible. To fully utilize the iron in your iron-fortified cereal, pair it with a citrus fruit or a glass of orange juice. Consider vitamin C to be the key that allows the body to absorb iron!

Variety Is Key: Avoid becoming bored with your cereal choices! Try out a variety of brands and varieties to determine which best fit your dietary requirements and palate. Seek cereals that have added fiber and whole grains to maximize your intake of other vital nutrients. Always keep in mind that variety adds flavor to life—this also holds true for the cereal you choose!

Watch Out for Sugar Monsters: Although some cereals with added iron are incredibly nutritious, others may be sugar monsters hiding in plain sight. Pay attention to added sugars, especially when it comes to kids. Choose natural sweeteners like fruit and cereals with less sugar. Consider it as picking the right side of the cereal aisle versus the wrong side!

Iron-Rich Cereals: A Progress Bar, Not a Finish Line Cereals fortified with iron are convenient and beneficial, but they shouldn't be your only source of iron. For a well-rounded nutritional strategy, investigate additional iron-rich foods such as lean meats, beans, lentils, and leafy greens. Recall that variety is essential for a long-term, healthy iron intake!

So welcome your handy allies on your iron quest: cereals fortified with iron! With every spoonful, they provide a tasty and useful way to increase your intake, promoting your overall wellbeing. Just watch the amount of sugar in them, make a variety of choices, and keep in mind that they are only a means to an end in your quest for ideal iron levels. Happy adventures in fortified iron!

Recall that these suggestions should not be used in place of expert medical advice; rather, they are intended to be educational and helpful. The best iron-rich options for your specific needs should always be determined in consultation with your healthcare provider.

Chapter 7:

Little Iron Powerhouses: Revealing the Secret Treasures in Nuts and Seeds

The powerful little heroes that lurk in the kingdom of nuts and seeds are not to be taken lightly! Despite being disregarded due to their small size, these little gems have a startling secret: they contain a powerful iron punch that can improve your health and power your days. So give up on the big weights and welcome the bite-sized iron champions!

Iron Warriors in Disguise: Nuts and seeds have a powerful iron content in addition to delicious flavors and crunchy textures. The iron kings, almonds, have 5 mg per ounce, and the creamy champions, cashews, have 6 mg. Pumpkin seeds, the zinc-iron duos, join the chorus with 1 mg per ounce, while chia seeds, the tiny titans, are iron warriors in disguise, offering 2 mg. Pistachios, hemp seeds, and even flax seeds join the chorus of the iron symphony, contributing a variety of flavors and iron-rich goodness.

Unlocking the Absorption Potential: Although these little powerhouses have a strong iron melody, your body may not be able to absorb its rhythm easily. Relax, the balance of nutrients holds the key! Citrus fruits, bell peppers, and tomatoes are rich in vitamin C, the master of iron absorption. When you combine these amazing vitamin C foods with your iron-rich nuts and seeds, you'll see the magic of absorption happen. Think of them as excited ushers, bringing the iron to the bloodstream's main platform.

Add Flavor to the Iron Symphony: Specific spices can also take center stage in the opera about iron absorption. The natural chelator curcumin found in turmeric increases the solubility and absorbability of iron. Piperine from black pepper joins the chorus, boosting iron absorption the way a backstage assistant shines the iron for a seamless transition into your system.

Beyond the Bowl of Snacks: Nuts and seeds are superfoods for more than just snacks!

Unleash their potential in the kitchen:

Salad Symphony: To add texture and nutrition to your salads, add chopped nuts and seeds.

Savory Sonata: For a nutty twist, add chopped nuts and seeds to pasta, curries, and stir-fries.

Smoothie Serenade: For a creamy, high-iron treat that can be consumed on the go, blend nuts and seeds into smoothies.

Baking Bonanza: For a tasty and nutritious twist, add ground nuts and seeds to baked goods like breads, muffins, and even pancakes.

Snack Symphony: Combine various nuts and seeds to create a portable, high-iron snack that will satisfy your cravings.

Recall:

Variety is essential. For a variety of nutrients and forms of iron, mix and match different nuts and seeds throughout the day.

Select options that are raw or dry-roasted: Skip the oil-roasted or salted varieties to reduce your intake of unhealthy fats and sodium.

Be mindful of the portion sizes: Nuts and seeds are high in calories even though they are nutritive foods. To get the most health benefits, enjoy them in moderation.

Consider your allergies: Make sure to select safe substitutes like hemp or sunflower seeds if you have any nut or seed allergies.

Raise your fork, then, to the powerful little heroes of the kingdom of nuts and seeds! These little powerhouses provide a tasty and easy way to increase your body's iron intake, nourish yourself, and infuse your meals with a little magic. Accept their many tastes, discover their adaptability, and witness the transformational force of these champions with a lot of iron!

Bonus Tip: To lessen phytic acid, a substance that can obstruct the absorption of iron, soak nuts and seeds overnight. Their complete iron-boosting potential can be unlocked with this easy step!

You can fully unleash the potential of the iron symphony concealed within nuts and seeds with a little imagination and these easy pointers. So enjoy every tasty, crunchy bite while nourishing your body with the iron-rich music!

○ **Iron Champions in Bite Size:**
Nuts and Seeds for Cooking
and Snacking

In the fast-paced field of nutrition, the little guys can sometimes be the strongest. Get ready to transform your eating and cooking habits with the iron-rich kingdom of nuts and seeds! Say goodbye to heavy protein bars and boring salads! These little giants are ready to fuel your days and improve your health without breaking the bank or your diet. They are bursting with flavor, texture, and of course, a powerful dose of iron. So embrace the bite-sized iron champions and throw off the monotony!

Don't be fooled by their size: Iron Symphony in Every Crunch. Nuts and seeds are iron powerhouses, strumming a varied tune of delicious iron-richness. Cashews, the creamy competitor, offer 6 mg per ounce, while almonds, the iron kings, lead the chorus at 5 mg. Pumpkin seeds, the zinc-iron duo, contribute 1 mg per ounce, while chia seeds, the little titans, contribute 2 mg. The harmony is completed by the addition of pistachios, hemp seeds, and even flaxseeds, which add a variety of flavors and iron-rich possibilities.

Unleashing the Absorption Magic: Although these little heroes have a powerful iron melody, your body may not be able to absorb their rhythm easily. But do not worry—nutrient harmony holds the key! Citrus fruits, bell peppers, and tomatoes are rich sources of vitamin C, which is a conductor of iron absorption. When you combine these amazing vitamin C foods with your iron-rich nuts and seeds, you'll see the magic of absorption happen. Think of them as excited ushers, bringing the iron to the bloodstream's main platform.

Add Flavor to the Iron Symphony: Specific spices can also take center stage in the opera about iron absorption. The natural chelator curcumin found in turmeric increases the solubility and absorbability of iron. Piperine from black pepper joins the chorus, boosting iron absorption the way a backstage assistant shines the iron for a seamless transition into your system.

Beyond the Bowl of Snacks: Nuts and seeds are superfoods for more than just snacks!

Unleash their potential in the kitchen:

Salad Symphony: To add texture and nutrition to your salads, add chopped nuts and seeds. For a traditional touch, try almonds and sunflower seeds; for a novel twist, try hemp seeds and pecans.

Savory Sonata: For a nutty twist, add chopped nuts and seeds to pasta, curries, and stir-fries. Walnuts and pumpkin seeds give stews and pastas a substantial crunch, while cashews and pine nuts give Asian-inspired cuisine a creamy richness.

Smoothie Serenade: For a creamy, high-iron treat that can be consumed on the go, blend nuts and seeds into smoothies. A smoothie with almond butter and chia seeds tastes like a rich dessert; a green smoothie with spinach and pistachios is a revitalizing and cool choice.

Baking Bonanza: For a tasty and nutritious twist, add ground nuts and seeds to baked goods like breads, muffins, and even pancakes. A gluten-free binder made of flaxseed meal can be used, and sunflower seeds give muffins and cookies a nutty sweetness.

Snack Symphony: Combine various nuts and seeds to create a portable, high-iron snack that will satisfy your cravings. For something sweet and salty, try a trail mix of cashews, cranberries, and pumpkin seeds. Alternatively, try something savory like roasted chickpeas, almonds, and spices.

Recall:

Variety is essential. For a variety of nutrients and forms of iron, mix and match different nuts

176

and seeds throughout the day. This keeps things lively and guarantees that your body absorbs all the health benefits of iron.

Select options that are raw or dry-roasted: Skip the oil-roasted or salted varieties to reduce your intake of unhealthy fats and sodium. Choosing raw or dry-roasted nuts and seeds allows you to maintain more flavor control and highlights their natural goodness.

Be mindful of the portion sizes: Nuts and seeds are high in calories even though they are nutritive foods. To get the most health benefits, enjoy them in moderation. A quarter-cup serving or a tiny handful is a reasonable amount to go by.

Consider your allergies: Make sure to select safe substitutes like hemp or sunflower seeds if you have any nut or seed allergies. Selecting options that are safe for you to enjoy is important because it shows that you value your health and well-being.

Raise your fork, then, to the powerful little heroes of the kingdom of nuts and seeds! These little titans provide a tasty and easy way to increase your body's iron intake, nourish yourself, and infuse your meals with a little magic. Accept their many tastes, discover their adaptability, and witness the transformational force of these champions with a lot of iron!

Recall that cooking and snacking ought to be pleasurable activities. Try out various combinations to see what you like best.

○ **Nut Butters and Seeds: Tasty Pairs for Activities to Increase Iron**

Forget monotonous iron-rich regimens and tasteless supplements! With every spoonful and sprinkle, the world of nut butters and seeds presents a colorful playground for your taste buds and a secret iron treasure trove, ready to power your days and improve your health. So, welcome these delectable duos as your new allies in the quest for iron-rich foods and throw off the monotony!

Iron Champions in Creamy Disguise: Nut butters have a smooth power that you should not undervalue. The iron king, almond butter, has 5 mg per ounce, and the creamy competitor, cashew butter, has 6 mg. The champion of sesame, tahini, contributes 2 mg per tablespoon to the chorus, and even the well-known favorite, peanut butter, adds 1 mg. The iron symphony doesn't stop there, though, as chia and sunflower seed butters offer different textures and a variety of delicious, iron-rich foods.

Unleashing the Absorption Magic: Although these creamy wonders have a strong iron melody, your body may not be able to absorb their rhythm easily. Relax, the balance of nutrients holds the key! Citrus fruits, bell peppers, and tomatoes are rich sources of vitamin C, which is a conductor of iron absorption. When you combine these vitamin C powerhouses with your nut butters and seeds, the magic of absorption will happen. Think of them as eager sous chefs who will infuse your food with flavor and elevate the iron to the forefront of your circulation.

Enhancing the Iron Symphony: Specific spices have the potential to take center stage in the opera of iron absorption. The natural chelator curcumin found in turmeric increases the solubility and absorbability of iron. Piperine from black pepper joins the chorus, boosting iron absorption the way a backstage assistant shines the iron for a seamless transition into your system.

Going Beyond Sandwich Spreads: Nut butters and seeds are friends for more than just toast!

Unleash their potential in the kitchen:

Savory Sonata: Add nut butters to dips and sauces to add a nutty, iron-rich punch. Stir-fries with an Asian flair are enhanced by the delicate sweetness of sunflower seed butter, and hummus is enhanced by the creamy depth of tahini.

Salad Symphony: To add a rich, creamy dressing to salads, drizzle nut butters over them. A zesty vinaigrette can be made with almond butter and lemon juice, and cashew butter elevates a simple green salad.

Smoothie Serenade: For a protein- and iron-rich on-the-go snack, blend nut butters and seeds into smoothies. Banana and peanut butter are a traditional combination, but chia seed pudding is a nutrient-dense, refreshing alternative.

Baking Bonanza: For a tasty and nutritious twist, incorporate nut butters and seeds into baked products such as muffins, breads, and even cookies. Granola bars get a delightful crunch from sunflower seeds, and tahini brownies are a decadent treat.

Snack Symphony: For a portable, high-iron snack, spread nut butters over apple slices or celery sticks. Add berries and nut butter to the top of rice cakes for a delightful midday snack.

Recall:

Variety is essential. To get a varied range of nutrients and forms of iron, mix and match different nut butters and seeds throughout the day. This guarantees that your body receives all of the advantages while also satisfying your taste buds.

Select natural alternatives: For the best possible health benefits, choose nut butters with little to no added sugar or oil. Keep in mind that making your own nut butters is a fantastic way to maintain ingredient control and savor the goodness of whole foods.

Be mindful of the portion sizes: Nut butters and seeds are high in calories, despite being delicious. To get the most health benefits, enjoy them in moderation. A quarter-cup of seeds and a tablespoon or two of nut butter are good starting points.

Consider your allergies: Select safe substitutes like tahini or sunflower seed butter if you have any nut or seed allergies. Selecting options that are safe for you to enjoy is important because it shows that you value your health and well-being.

Raise your spoon to the tantalizing pairings of seeds and nut butters! These crunchy allies and creamy champions provide a tasty and practical way to up your iron intake, nourish your body, and infuse your meals with a little magic. Accept their many tastes, discover their adaptability, and witness the transformational force of these allies rich in iron!

Keep in mind that including nut butters and seeds in your diet is a process rather than a final goal. Try different things until you find what works for you, and have fun while doing it. Happy iron-boosting travels!

○ **Combining Nuts and Seeds with Other Iron Powerhouses to Unleash the Iron Symphony**

Iron is a key component of nutrition, contributing vital melody and supplying oxygen to your cells to keep you energized. However, for solo instruments such as nuts and seeds to shine, there sometimes needs to be some harmony. Step forward, a varied cast of iron-rich friends, prepared to up your daily iron intake and produce a delicious and healthful symphony!

Nuts & Seeds: The Crispy Lead:

Almonds: Packed with 5 milligrams per ounce, these iron kings are a powerful addition to any dish.

Cashews: These smooth, creamy crooners are perfect for adding to smoothies or sauces because they have a smooth 6 mg per ounce.

Pumpkin Seeds: These little gems contribute 1 mg of zinc and iron per ounce, giving both minerals a boost and a delightful crunch.

Chia Seeds: These tiny powerhouses, containing 2 milligrams per ounce, are so adaptable that they can be added to salads or soaked into puddings.

Vitamin C: The Absorption Conductor

Even though seeds and nuts sing their iron melody, your body may not be able to easily absorb their rhythm. Do not be alarmed; vitamin C, the energetic conductor, is about to take the stage! Vitamin C makes iron shine brightly in citrus fruits, bell peppers, and tomatoes. It increases absorption of iron and makes sure your body gets the benefits of every crunchy bite.

Add Some Flavor to the Symphony:

In the iron absorption opera, some spices can also take center stage. Curcumin from turmeric acts as a natural chelator, increasing iron solubility, and piperine from black pepper improves absorption like a backstage worker polishing iron for a polished entrance.

Beyond the Bowl of Snacks:

Nuts and seeds are not one-man shows!

Allow them to harmonize with other stars rich in iron:

Leafy Greens: With up to 6 mg per cup, spinach, kale, and collard greens are iron powerhouses that join the chorus. Blend them into nutrient-dense green smoothies along with nuts and seeds.

Beans and Lentils: These iron-rich superstars, which provide 6–8 mg per cooked cup, pair well with nuts and seeds in salads, stews, and even burgers to form a substantial and high-protein partnership.

Lean Meat and Poultry: Heme iron is easily absorbed by the body and is found in chicken, beef, and turkey. It combines powerfully with non-heme iron found in nuts and seeds. A tasty and high-iron meal to try is a stir-fry with chicken, cashews, and peppers.

With 2-3 mg of iron per serving, tofu and tempeh are plant-based protein sources that go well with nuts and seeds in stir-fries, curries, and even vegan meatballs.

Recall:

Variety is essential. Throughout the day, alternate between various iron sources to make sure your body gets a variety of iron forms and nutrients.

Control of portions: Nuts, seeds, and other sources can be high in calories but also high in iron. To get the most health benefits, enjoy them in moderation.

Be cautious of absorption inhibitors: Some foods, such as tea and coffee, can prevent the body from absorbing iron. Eat them in moderation or at different times from meals high in iron.

Speak with a medical professional: Always get advice from a trained healthcare professional if you have any concerns about your iron levels.

Now, lift your fork to enjoy the magnificent iron symphony! Nuts and seeds create a delicious and nutritious melody that nourishes your body and powers your days when combined with other iron-rich powerhouses. Savor the variety of tastes, experiment with inventive recipes, and discover the harmonious transformational potential of iron!

Never forget that maintaining optimal iron levels requires eating a healthy, balanced diet.

Nuts and seeds are great allies, but to make sure your body gets all the nutrients it needs to thrive, you also need to include a variety of sources that are high in iron. Cheers to good food and iron-boosting travels!

Part 3:

Opening the Iron Symphony: A Manual for the Best Absorption

Iron, your body's essential oxygen conductor, merits a platform befitting its strength. However, due to inadequate absorption, this vital mineral can occasionally disappear behind the scenes. Do not panic, iron seekers! This guide will help you maximize the amount of iron that your body absorbs and make sure that every meal is a vibrant melody of health.

The Absorption Orchestra: Iron absorption is a melodic dance performed by a skilled group of supporting actors and the soloist **(food high in iron)**:

Vitamin C: The star conductor that steals the show, vitamin C is found in citrus fruits, bell peppers, and tomatoes. It binds to non-heme iron, which is found in plant sources, and directs it toward the center of the body for absorption.

Heme Iron: The star of the show, heme iron is easily absorbed by your body and doesn't require vitamin C to do so. It can be found in meat, poultry, and seafood.

Spices: Turmeric and black pepper, the backstage crew, work as organic chelators to get iron ready for absorption.

Bringing the melody into harmony:

Mix & Match: Iron need not be an isolated piece! Eat foods high in vitamin C along with plant-based iron sources like lentils, beans, and leafy greens for a potent absorption boost. Imagine a stir-fried bean and pepper dish or a lentil salad with chopped oranges.

Befriend Heme Iron: For a well-rounded symphony, incorporate moderate amounts of heme iron sources with plant-based iron.

Complementary dishes like salmon salad with spinach or quinoa with added iron can be enjoyed together.

Elevate the Presentation: Incorporate a dash of black pepper and turmeric into your meals high in iron. These spices ensure that the conductor and soloist perform in perfect harmony by improving taste as well as iron absorption.

Breaking Through Absorption Barriers:

Tea and coffee are popular drinks that, although delicious, can bind to iron and prevent absorption. Eat them in moderation or at different times from meals high in iron.

Calcium Overload: Dairy products can compete with iron for absorption despite being high in calcium. For best results, spread out your iron- and calcium-rich meals throughout the day.

Phytates: Phytates are present in some grains, legumes, and seeds and have the ability to bind iron. These foods can benefit from soaking, sprouting, or fermenting in order to lower phytates and increase iron bioavailability.

Past the Snack:

Cook with Caution: Overcooking can reduce the amount of iron in foods that are high in iron, such as vegetables. Use gentle cooking techniques to protect the priceless mineral, such as stir-frying or steaming.

Pay Attention to Your Body: Age, gender, and health conditions all influence how much iron is needed. For individualized guidance, speak with a healthcare provider if you have concerns about your iron levels.

Honor Diversity: Avoid getting into a rut! To make sure your body gets a variety of nutrients and forms of iron, try a wide range of foods high in iron.
Recall that iron absorption is a team effort. Meals can become iron-rich symphonies that

fuel your body and your days if you know the supporting players and get past any obstacles. Raise your fork, eat like a maestro, and discover the life-changing potential of optimal iron absorption!

Bonus Tip: Fatigue, low energy, and trouble concentrating are just a few of the subtle ways that an iron deficiency can show up. If you notice any of these symptoms, get in touch with a medical expert for an accurate diagnosis and course of action. You can make sure your iron symphony plays on, loud and clear, with a little awareness and these useful tips!

Chapter 8:

Food Pairing: Iron Absorption's Covert Weapon

The vital component of your cells, iron, is frequently overlooked in gastronomic chaos. It's whispered in the crunch of nuts and seeds, nestled inside lentils, and buried in leafy greens. Iron warriors, do not be afraid! Food pairing, the iron-rich symphony of meals, is here to help you fully utilize this essential mineral. It's the secret weapon of absorption.

Vitamin C and Iron, the Dynamic Duo Think of iron as a timid soloist who is afraid to take the lead. Enterprising conductor vitamin C intervenes by binding with non-heme iron **(found in plants)** and directing it into the center of your bloodstream. Bell peppers, tomatoes, and citrus fruits form a vibrant chorus that increases the absorption of iron. Imagine a spinach smoothie with a hint of orange or a lentil salad dressed with a zesty vinaigrette.

The Heme Advantage: The superstar of the iron world is heme iron, which can be found in meat, poultry, and seafood. It easily marches onto the absorption stage without the need for a vitamin C escort. However, don't write off the rising stars of the plant-based world! Even so, heme iron and foods high in vitamin C can work in harmony to improve the absorption of both forms of iron. An excellent illustration of this well-balanced combination is chicken stir-fried with peppers and broccoli.

Enhancing the Absorption: Black pepper and turmeric are not only kitchen staples; they also serve as backstage crew members, getting iron ready for absorption. Iron's hold on binding agents is loosened by the natural chelator curcumin found in turmeric. Piperine from black pepper adds its magical touch, amplifying iron absorption like a spotlight operator lighting the main act. When you add these spices to your iron-rich meals, you'll see a magical increase in absorption.

Beyond the Pairings: Simple duos are just the beginning of the food pairing orchestra.

This is the method for composing entire iron symphonies:

A powerful source of iron and vitamin C can be made with a salad serenade made with spinach, lentils, and chopped oranges. For a final taste and absorbency, add a sprinkling of sunflower seeds and a dressing flavored with turmeric.

Smoothie Orchestra: Blend berries, chia seeds, and pumpkin seeds to make a creamy, iron-rich treat. To increase the amount of vitamin C and make a nutrient-dense masterpiece, add a squeeze of lemon or a dash of green powder.

Stir-frying Sonata: For a tasty and iron-rich stir-fry, sauté tofu, broccoli, and peppers with ginger and garlic. For an enhanced absorption, culminate by adding a dash of black pepper and a squeeze of lime.

Recall:

Variety Is Essential: Avoid becoming mired in a pairing rut! Try varying the proportions of foods high in iron and sources of vitamin C to make sure your body gets a variety of nutrients and forms of iron.

Moderation Is Important: Even though they are delicious, some combinations might need some harmony. Eat fewer calcium-rich dairy products with meals high in iron because calcium can impede the absorption of iron.

Be Aware of the Inhibitors: Although they are popular drinks, coffee and tea can bind to iron and prevent absorption. Eat them in moderation or at different times from meals high in iron.

Pay Attention to Your Body: Age, gender, and health conditions all influence how much iron is needed. For individualized guidance, speak with a healthcare provider if you have concerns about your iron levels.

Food pairing is a scientific symphony designed to maximize the benefits of iron, not just a matter of culinary artistry. With each delectable bite, you can transform your meals into iron-rich masterpieces that fuel your days and nourish your body by comprehending the supporting players and overcoming any obstacles. Raise your fork, eat like a maestro, and discover how food pairing can optimize the absorption of iron in your body!

Bonus Tip: Reduced phytate levels in germinated grains and legumes can enhance iron absorption. For an additional iron boost, think about including sprouted grains or soaked lentils in your diet.

You can turn your kitchen into a stage for iron absorption with a little imagination and these practical suggestions, making sure your body gets the iron symphony it needs to flourish!

○ **Iron Symphony: Using Vitamin C Boosters to Harmonize Your Meals**

Iron, the conductor of oxygen in your body, merits a platform commensurate with its strength. However, occasionally inadequate absorption causes this essential mineral to disappear behind the scenes. Iron warriors, do not be afraid! With the help of vitamin C enhancers and iron-rich foods, you can create a vibrant melody of health with every bite. These nutrients are like the enthusiastic conductors of the iron absorption orchestra.

Consider iron to be a timid soloist who is afraid to take the lead in The Absorption Opera. Enter the stage left by Vitamin C, the conductor who steals the show! Vitamin C, which is present in bell peppers, tomatoes, citrus fruits, and even berries, binds to non-heme iron, which is present in plants, and moves it to the front of the absorption chain. This melodic pair maximizes the benefits of plant-based iron and guarantees that your body gets the essential oxygen it requires.

The Enhancer Ensemble: There is a varied group of vitamin C enhancers that are waiting to join the iron symphony beyond the bright lights of citrus:

Tangy Tomatoes: These adaptable fruits (yes, fruits!) go well with leafy greens, lentils, and beans. They also have a good amount of vitamin C. For a robust, iron-rich balance, consider a tomato and lentil soup.

Powerhouse Bell Pepper: Any color of bell pepper—green, red, or yellow—adds a vibrant burst of vitamin C and goes great with stir-fries, tofu, and chicken. Stir-frying red pepper and tofu is a vibrant, iron-rich duet.

Berry Bonanza: These delectable, tart, and sweet treats are more than just dessert; they also contain a surprisingly high amount of vitamin

C. For an iron and vitamin C boost, blend them into smoothies with spinach or add them to oatmeal mixed with nuts and seeds.

Tropical Twists: Rich in vitamin C, papaya, mango, and pineapple add a hint of the tropics to your diet. Savor them with grilled fish that is high in iron or in a salad with quinoa for a light and healthy lunch.

Beyond the Plate: Keep in mind that your meals are only the beginning of the iron symphony:

Drink a glass of freshly squeezed orange juice to start your day, or squeeze some lemon or lime into your water as you go. These easy routines maintain the vitamin C conductor in the spotlight, prepared to direct iron whenever it enters.

Medicinal Harmonies: Herbs like parsley, cilantro, and even mint give your iron-rich dishes a welcome burst of vitamin C. Imagine adding some chopped parsley to a lentil stew or adding mint to a smoothie to boost its iron content.

Add some flare to the Symphony: Don't overlook the backstage staff! Black pepper and turmeric improve iron absorption, which gives the iron soloist more self-assurance on stage. To enhance the absorption of your meals, sprinkle them on top.

Balance in Each Bite:

Mix and Match: Steer clear of formulaic pairings! Try varying the amounts of foods high in iron and supplements high in vitamin C to make sure your body gets a variety of nutrients and iron in different forms.

Moderation Is Important: Even though they are delicious, some combinations might need some harmony. Eat fewer calcium-rich dairy products with meals high in iron because calcium can impede the absorption of iron.

Be Aware of the Inhibitors: Although they are popular drinks, coffee and tea can bind to iron and prevent absorption. Eat them in moderation or at different times from meals high in iron.

Pay Attention to Your Body: Age, gender, and health conditions all influence how much iron is needed. For individualized guidance, speak with a healthcare provider if you have concerns about your iron levels.

Your meals can become iron-rich symphonies if you embrace a variety of pairings and are aware of the power of vitamin C enhancers. Raise your fork, eat with grace, and discover the transformative power of food for the best possible absorption of iron! Recall that the key to maximizing the benefits of this essential mineral is to eat a healthy, balanced diet that emphasizes foods high in iron and foods that boost vitamin C levels. This will guarantee that your body gets the vibrant melody of health with every mouthwatering bite.

○ **The Iron Symphony: A Chorus of Nutrients Boosts Absorption Beyond Vitamin C**

As your body's oxygen conductor, iron merits a magnificent orchestra to emphasize its essential function. As the conductor of iron absorption, vitamin C certainly has the upper hand, but there are plenty of other skilled performers on the stage who all play their parts to create a beautiful symphony of ideal iron uptake. Let's examine the various functions these nutrients perform in guaranteeing your body gets the iron it requires to function properly.

The Rhythm Section: Crucial Companions

Copper: This vital trace mineral maintains the iron rhythm by acting as a skilled percussionist. Copper plays a role in the metabolism of iron, moving it from storage into your blood. Consider it the backstage staff making sure the iron soloist is prepared for its big moment.

Vitamin B12: This multipurpose vitamin contributes to the production of red blood cells and the utilization of iron, joining the melody as a backing vocalist. The iron solo might have trouble achieving its maximum potential in the absence of B12. Consider it the sound engineer, making sure the intended audience hears the message on the iron.

Folic acid: This essential B vitamin gives the chorus depth and is essential for the synthesis of red blood cells and the absorption of iron. Folic acid ensures the impact of the iron symphony by acting as its harmony vocals.

The Ensemble of Supporting Cast: Inhibitors and Enhancers:

Protein: Lean protein, such as fish or chicken, works as a helpful spotlight to improve the absorption of iron from plant-based sources. Consider it as the lighting on the stage, highlighting and increasing the audience's visibility of the iron soloist.

Spices: By increasing iron solubility and bioavailability, backstage technicians like turmeric and black pepper improve iron absorption. Consider them to be the audio technicians, making sure the message on the iron is audible and clear.

Phytates: Phytates, which are present in grains, legumes, and seeds, can function as stagehands by obstructing the entrance of the iron soloist. These foods can be made more absorbable by soaking, sprouting, or fermenting, which lowers their phytate content.

Calcium: Although necessary, calcium may compete with iron for absorption. Consume dairy products high in calcium at different times from meals high in iron to prevent competition and make sure each nutrient has its due.

Leading the Symphony:

Variety is essential. Stay out of the solo act! Incorporate a variety of iron-rich foods into your diet, such as meat, beans, lentils, and leafy greens, to make sure you get a range of iron forms and complementary nutrients.

Moderation is important. It's important to maintain balance. Certain nutrients can help the body absorb iron better than others. In order to achieve a harmonious symphony of optimal nutrition, enjoy each food group in moderation.

Recognize your inhibitors: Take into consideration things like tea and coffee, which can bind to iron and decrease absorption. Eat them in moderation or at different times from meals high in iron.

Pay attention to your body. Age, gender, and health conditions all influence how much iron is needed. Seek individualized advice from a healthcare professional if you are concerned about your iron levels.

Past the Snack:

Cook carefully: Low-heat cooking techniques, such as steaming or stir-frying, help to retain the iron content of food. Steer clear of overcooking, as this can reduce the bioavailability of iron.

Accept fermentation: By making more iron and other nutrients available, foods like kimchi and yogurt that have undergone fermentation can enhance the absorption of iron.

Pay attention to your intuition: An iron-absorbing gut microbiome is important. Incorporate prebiotics and probiotics into your diet to help maintain the health of your gut.

Recall that iron absorption is a team effort. You can arrange your foods to provide a harmonious balance of the best possible iron absorption by knowing the various functions of other nutrients, enhancers, and inhibitors. Now lift your fork, conduct your meals with mastery, and discover the transforming power of a masterfully conducted iron symphony!

Bonus Advice: Remember the importance of staying hydrated! Water is essential for the absorption of nutrients, including iron. To guarantee that the iron symphony plays to its fullest extent, make sure you drink enough water throughout the day.

You can make sure your body gets the essential iron it needs to power your days and create a symphony of health with every bite by implementing these suggestions and appreciating the varied chorus of nutrients that support iron absorption!

○ Meal Planning and Food Pairing: A Delectable Nutritional Symphony

Meal preparation and food pairing are secret weapons in your toolbox for maximizing your health and wellbeing—they're not just about taste and convenience! You can arrange colorful symphonies of flavor and nutritional synergy on your plate by learning how different foods interact with one another. Put on your chef's hat and join me as we discuss useful strategies for converting your meals from basic nourishment to delectable creations that will delight your senses and benefit your body!

Organizing Your Chef's Concerto:

Variety adds flavor to both life and food! Avoid becoming mired in a culinary rut! Try to fill your plate with as many different kinds of fruits, vegetables, whole grains, and lean proteins as you can each week. By doing this, you can be sure that your body is getting a variety of vitamins, minerals, and antioxidants to keep it healthy.

Seasonal melodies: Enjoy the abundance of every season! Seasonal and locally grown produce is often at its best in terms of flavor and nutrition. It's also an affordable way to lessen your carbon footprint and give back to your community.

Combine it all: Meal preparation and planning ahead of time saves time and helps you avoid making bad decisions at the last minute. Make a big pot of quinoa or brown rice to use throughout the week, or roast veggies in bulk for quick salads and stir-fries.

Food Pairing: The Nutrient Harmony

In the realm of nutrients, vitamin C and iron are a classic pair that hold great power! Vitamin C improves the absorption of nonheme iron **(plant-based iron)** from beans, lentils, and leafy greens. Vitamin C can be found in citrus fruits, bell peppers, and tomatoes. Imagine a lentil soup with a chopped tomato topping or spinach salad dressed with a zesty vinaigrette.

Iron from plants and protein: Fish or chicken are examples of lean protein that can work like a spotlight to increase the absorption of iron from plant-based sources. For a filling and high-iron dinner, try a lentil and chicken stew or a tofu stir-fry served with brown rice.

Spices that aid in absorption: Never undervalue the influence of spices! Due to their increased solubility, black pepper and turmeric improve iron absorption. For an added flavor boost and extra absorption boost, sprinkle them over your iron-rich dishes.

Past the Pairings:

Liven up your life by experimenting with different herbs and spices! Not only do they enhance taste, but they also have several health advantages. Try a Thai stir-fry with ginger and garlic, or a lentil salad Moroccan-style with cumin and coriander.

Use your imagination when preparing leftovers: You don't have to eat boring leftovers! Turn them into intriguing new recipes. Roasted vegetables can be added to soups or omelets, and leftover chicken can be used as a salad topper.

Turn it into a family event: Include the people you care about in the planning and preparation of meals. Together with teaching kids about good nutrition, this is a wonderful way to make enduring culinary memories.

Recall that meal planning and food pairing are about discovering tasty and healthful options rather than following strict rules! Accept the harmony of tastes and nutrients, try out various pairings, and most of all, enjoy yourself in the kitchen!

Here are a few more pointers to remember:

Recognize your inhibitors: Some foods, such as tea and coffee, can prevent the body from absorbing iron. Eat them in moderation or at different times from meals high in iron.

Pay attention to your body. Take note of your feelings after eating various foods. Modify your meals based on what you find disagreeable.

Remember the enjoyable factor! Planning meals and matching foods ought to be fun! To keep things interesting, choose foods you enjoy and try experimenting with different flavors and textures.

With the help of these culinary hacks, you can turn your meals into nutrient-dense symphonies that will power your days and nourish your body with every delicious bite! To create a culinary masterpiece that speaks to your health and well-being, pick up your apron, lift your fork, and maestro your meals!

Chapter 9:

Opening the Iron Symphony: Preserving the Precious Mineral through Cooking Methods

The vital component of your cells, iron, is frequently overlooked in gastronomic chaos. Elevated temperature, acidic surroundings, and excessive cooking can steal its essential melody, leaving you with a nutritional tune that is muted. Iron warriors, do not be afraid! This guide is your key to using mindful cooking to fully utilize the benefits of this priceless mineral and make sure your meals are harmoniously rich in iron.

The Heat Wave: Iron requires careful handling, just like a delicate aria. Iron can be oxidized and degraded by high heat, which will weaken the melody.

Choose kinder techniques like:

Steaming: This keeps your iron solo crisp and clear while preserving flavor and nutrients. To keep the iron in fish, broccoli, and leafy greens intact, steam them.

Stir-frying: Lean meats, tofu, and vegetables retain iron best when cooked in short bursts over high heat with little to no oil.

Poaching: This gentle cooking technique minimizes iron loss by cooking food in a simmering liquid, perfect for eggs and fish.

The Acidic Chorus: The melody can be muted by certain acidic ingredients that bind with iron. While citrus fruits are excellent for absorbing iron when combined with foods high in iron, avoid using them while cooking:

Lessen the acidity: When cooking foods high in iron, use neutral cooking liquids like water or broth. If using tomatoes, use low-acid types or balance the acidity with a small amount of baking soda.

Seasonality with strategy: Spices and herbs like turmeric, ginger, and garlic can be used to enhance flavor without lowering iron content. When cooking, stay away from acidic spices like vinegar and lemon pepper.

Cookware is important. While cast iron cookware is a great way to add iron to your food, acidic foods can also absorb iron from it. To avoid losing iron, use enameled cast iron or stainless steel for acidic dishes.

The Opera of Overcooking: Your iron solo may not succeed if you leave it up on stage for too long. Iron is destroyed and its bioavailability is decreased by overcooking.

Recall:

Less is more. Grain and vegetable textures should be al dente, and meat should only be cooked until it is just tender to prevent overcooking and iron loss.

Continued cooking: Benefit from leftover cooking! Foods should be taken off the heat a little before they are done so that the residual heat can gently finish cooking them.

Save your leftovers for later: Avoid reheating foods high in iron too frequently. To prevent further iron deficiency, reheat only the necessary amount.

Beyond the Range Top:

Soaking and sprouting: Phytates, which are found in grains, legumes, and seeds, can prevent the absorption of iron. Iron bioavailability can be increased and phytate levels can be decreased by soaking or sprouting them.

Fermentation: By making iron and other nutrients more readily available, fermented foods like kimchi and yogurt can improve the absorption of iron.

Storage is important. Foods high in iron should be kept in sealed containers to avoid oxidation and maintain their nutritional content.

Recall that careful preparation rather than restriction is the key to cooking for iron preservation. You can cook like a maestro and make sure every bite of your iron symphony resounds with health and vibrant nutrition by knowing the effects of heat, acidity, and cooking time.

Bonus Tip: You can further improve iron absorption by including foods high in vitamin C, such as bell peppers, citrus fruits, or tomatoes, in your iron-rich meals. This will turn your dish into a true nutritional masterpiece!

With these thoughtful cooking techniques, you can unleash the full potential of iron, so lift up your spatula and maestro your meals. Allow iron to take center stage in your kitchen, singing a scrumptious and nourishing tune that feeds your body and your spirit!

○ Iron Symphony: Preserving Your Meals' Priceless Melody

As your body's oxygen conductor, iron deserves a colorful orchestra of scrumptious and nourishing foods to emphasize its important function. However, iron can lose its tone when cooked, much like a delicate instrument, leaving your health on the dull side. Iron warriors, do not be afraid! Your secret to reducing iron loss and creating dishes that sing with iron-rich harmony is this guide.

The Acid and the Heat: Think of iron as a sensitive soloist. Elevated body temperature and acidic surroundings may overshadow it, reducing its bioavailability.

Here's how to maintain its prominence:

Accept the gentle touch: Steer clear of high-heat techniques like grilling or frying and instead use steaming, simmering, or poaching. These kinder methods maintain the iron melody, ensuring that your eggs, fish, and leafy greens retain their essential melody.

Reduce the acidic chorus by using ingredients that bind with iron, such as tomatoes, which will muffle the song. When cooking, keep them to a minimum and use low-acid varieties whenever you can. The acidity can also be neutralized with a small pinch of baking soda.

Enhance the harmony by substituting savory spices like garlic, ginger, and turmeric for acidic ones like vinegar. These give your dish more depth without lowering the iron content, so it remains colorful and nutrient-dense.

The Opera of Overcooking: Your iron soloist may fail if you keep it on stage for too long. Iron is destroyed by overcooking, and its bioavailability is also decreased.

Recall:

For pasta or veggies, aim for al dente, which is a slightly firm texture. This guarantees an appealing bite and maximum nutrient retention.

The secret to carryover cooking: harness the heat that remains! Your iron-rich dish will finish cooking more gently if you remove it from the heat a little before desired doneness. This maintains the iron melody without sacrificing texture or flavor.

Even leftovers can sing: Steer clear of reheating foods high in iron multiple times. To avoid further iron deficiency, gently reheat the amount you require.

Beyond the Range Top: There are ways to keep the iron symphony resounding even when the heat is off:

Maintaining adequate hydration is essential as it facilitates the body's absorption of various nutrients, including iron. Drink plenty of water and allow the iron melody to flow.

Soak and sprout: Phytates, which are found in grains, legumes, and seeds, can prevent the absorption of iron. They can absorb more iron and have their phytate levels lowered by soaking or sprouting.

Friends of fermentation: Fermented foods, such as kimchi and yogurt, increase the body's availability of iron, which improves absorption. When you incorporate them into your meals, the iron chorus will work in unison with other nutrients.

Keep in mind that careful planning rather than restriction is the key to reducing iron loss during cooking. You can become the conductor of your meals by learning how heat, acidity, and cooking time affect them. This will guarantee that every bite of your iron symphony is full of health and vibrant nutrition.

Bonus Tip: Iron absorption is aided by vitamin C like a bright light! The iron melody is amplified and a truly nutritious masterpiece is created when vitamin C-rich fruits and vegetables, such as bell peppers, citrus fruits, or tomatoes, are combined with iron-rich foods.

Now lift that spatula, cook like a maestro, and use these deliberate actions to maximize the benefits of iron. Allow iron to take center stage in your kitchen, creating a scrumptious and nourishing symphony that nourishes and powers your days with every delicious note!

○ **Unlocking Taste and Nutrition: A Handbook for Selecting the Best Cooking Techniques**

Cooking is a vibrant dance between heat, time, and ingredients that turns raw materials into culinary masterpieces. It's about more than just feeding a hunger. However, there are so many different cooking techniques that picking the best one can be like navigating a maze. Do not be afraid, fellow gastronomic explorers! Your key to unlocking the mysteries of each technique is this guide, which will guarantee that you cook delectable meals while preserving the priceless nutrients concealed in your ingredients.

The Symphony of Flavors: Every cooking technique adds a different note to the overall harmony of your food.

Let's investigate a few of the primary instruments:

The Searing Solo: Using high heat, such as grilling or pan-frying, results in a gorgeous caramelized crust that seals in juices and flavor on meats and vegetables. For stir-fries, steaks, and chops, this technique works great, but keep in mind that prolonged searing can reduce some of the nutrients.

The Gentle Duet: Poaching and simmering gradually extract the essence of ingredients without undermining their fragile structures, much like two birds singing in unison. Their mild touch brings out the best in soups, stews, and poached fish, preserving vitamins and minerals for a filling palate.

The Serenade of Steam: Using only water vapor to cook food while maintaining its original color, texture, and nutritional value, steaming is the minimalist maestro. Under the gentle touch of this method, leafy greens, delicate seafood, and dumplings sing their praises.

The Baking Ballad: Baking turns basic dough into fluffy breads, rich cakes, and flavorful casseroles. It also produces a symphony of scents and textures. Although it's not always the best way to retain nutrients, baking provides a special way to include fruits, vegetables, and whole grains in your diet.

The Harmonious Nutrients: But the preservation of the priceless nutrients that fuel our bodies is the true purpose of cooking—it's not just about flavor.

Here's how to pick the best approach for the best possible nutrition:

Heat and Vitamin C: High temperatures can affect vitamin C, an essential antioxidant. For fruits and vegetables high in this vitamin, such as broccoli, berries, and citrus fruits, use gentler preparation techniques like steaming or poaching.

Fat and Fat-Soluble Vitamins: Consuming healthy fats with vitamins A, D, E, and K optimizes their absorption. When cooking with nuts, avocado oil, or olive oil in moderation, the vitamins from vegetables and fatty fish are better absorbed.

Minerals and Overcooking: In general, minerals that are cooked, such as iron and magnesium, stay stable. Overcooking, however, can still reduce their bioavailability. Lean meats and seafood should not be overcooked; instead, aim for al dente textures for pasta and grains.

Beyond the Fundamentals: The fundamentals are just the beginning of your culinary adventure!

Here are some more pointers for optimizing nutrition and flavor:

Accept the rainbow: Include a range of vibrant fruits and vegetables in your diet. With different colors denoting different nutrients, a varied plate guarantees your body a varied nutritional symphony.

Make friends with herbs and spices: Not only do spices and herbs improve flavor, but they are also a great source of antioxidants and other health-promoting ingredients. Try varying the combinations to enhance the nutritional value of your food while giving it more depth and complexity.

Pay attention to your ingredients: Different methods work for different foods. To guarantee the best outcomes and nutrient retention, pay close attention to the texture and cooking time of each ingredient.

Keep in mind that cooking is an exquisite voyage of exploration, with you acting as the guide. You can turn your meals into gastronomic masterpieces that sing with flavor and nourish your body with every delectable bite by learning the special advantages of each cooking technique and placing a high priority on nutrient preservation. Now lift that whisk, conductor of ingredients, and cook up culinary symphonies of flavor and health!

Extra Advice: Never underestimate the power of leftovers! Repurposing leftovers into novel and intriguing recipes reduces food waste and optimizes nutrient utilization. Go wild with your culinary imagination and get creative!

Have fun on your culinary explorations and never forget that love is always the most crucial component!

- **Iron Symphony: Crafting Wholesome Dishes with Each Bite**

The vital component of your cells, iron, is frequently overlooked in gastronomic chaos. It's easy to miss, buried in leafy greens, tucked away in lentils, and whispered in the crunch of nuts and seeds. Iron warriors, do not be afraid! With the help of this guide, you can fully utilize the benefits of this essential mineral and turn every delicious bite of food into an iron-rich symphony.

Organizing the Iron Feast:

Accept the rainbow: It's all about variety! Avoid becoming mired in a culinary rut. Aim for a rainbow of colors on your plate by including foods high in iron from various food groups, such as beans, lentils, leafy greens, and lean meats. This guarantees that you get a variety of iron forms and beneficial nutrients.

Seasonal melodies: Seasonal and locally grown produce frequently has the best flavor and nutrition content. It's also affordable and gives back to the community. Thus, allow the changing of the seasons to direct your iron symphony by adding juicy berries to summer smoothies or thick stews made with winter veggies.

Combine it all: Meal preparation and planning ahead of time saves time and helps you avoid making bad decisions at the last minute. Make a big pot of quinoa or brown rice to use throughout the week, or roast a bunch of veggies for quick stir-fries and salads.

Combining for the Best Absorption:

Iron and vitamin C together are a powerful duo that accentuate the iron note! Vitamin C improves the absorption of nonheme iron **(plant-based iron)** from beans, lentils, and leafy greens. Vitamin C can be found in citrus fruits, bell peppers, and tomatoes. Imagine a lentil soup with a chopped tomato topping or spinach salad dressed with a zesty vinaigrette.

Iron from plants and protein: Fish or chicken are examples of lean protein that can work like a spotlight to increase the absorption of iron from plant-based sources. For a filling and high-iron dinner, try a lentil and chicken stew or a tofu stir-fry served with brown rice.

Spices that aid in absorption: Never undervalue the influence of spices! Due to their increased solubility, black pepper and turmeric improve iron absorption. For an added flavor boost and extra absorption boost, sprinkle them over your iron-rich dishes.

Past the Pairings:

Be aware of the inhibitors: Tea and coffee are two foods that can prevent the body from absorbing iron. Eat them in moderation or at different times from meals high in iron.

Pay attention to your body. Take note of your feelings after eating various foods. Modify your meals based on what you find disagreeable.

Turn it into a family event: Include the people you care about in the planning and preparation of meals. Together with teaching kids about good nutrition, this is a wonderful way to make enduring culinary memories.

Cooking to Keep the Most Iron in Your Food:

Low heat: Iron can be oxidized and degraded by high heat. For foods high in iron, such as fish, eggs, and leafy greens, use gentler cooking techniques like steaming, simmering, or poaching.

Acidic balance: Iron can bind with some acidic substances. When cooking, keep them to a minimum and use low-acid types whenever you can. Another useful tool for balancing acidity is a pinch of baking soda.

Less is more. Grain and vegetable textures should be al dente, and to prevent iron loss, meat should only be cooked until it is just tender. Keep in mind that carryover cooking permits a gentle final cooking by residual heat.

Extra Advice:

By soaking and sprouting, grains, legumes, and seeds lose some of their phytates, which can impede the absorption of iron.

Fermentation: By making iron and other nutrients more readily available, fermented foods like kimchi and yogurt can improve the absorption of iron.

Even leftovers can sing: Avoid reheating foods high in iron more than once. To prevent further iron deficiency, reheat only the necessary amount.

Recall that cooking meals and following iron-rich recipes is about making thoughtful decisions rather than about restriction. You can turn your meals into symphonies of deliciousness and nutrition by understanding the effects of food pairings, cooking methods, and nutrient interactions. This will guarantee that your body gets the essential iron it needs to thrive. Raise your fork, eat with grace, and discover the transformative power of food for the best possible absorption of iron!

You can create culinary masterpieces in your kitchen that will fuel your days and nourish your body with every delicious bite by using these tips and a little creativity!

Chapter 10:

Unlocking the Iron Melody: Getting Past Absorption Obstacles

As your body's oxygen conductor, iron merits a platform befitting its strength. However, some people may lose track of this essential mineral due to inadequate absorption. Iron warriors, do not be afraid! With the help of this guide, you can recognize and overcome common absorption obstacles and make sure that every meal delivers the lively melody of health to your body.

Making the Absorption Blues Diagnosis:

Symptoms: Iron deficiency can manifest as weakness, fatigue, pale skin, shortness of breath, and cold hands and feet. But hold off on drawing conclusions! For an accurate diagnosis, including blood tests to determine iron levels and the root cause of your absorption difficulties, speak with your healthcare provider.

Typical offenders: Iron absorption can be hampered by a few medical conditions, including Crohn's disease, celiac disease, and heavy menstruation. Dietary variables that may also be important include consuming too much coffee or tea, insufficient vitamin C, and low intake of foods high in iron.

Styling the Absorption Symphony in Harmony:

Food First: Give iron-rich foods top priority! Choose a variety of foods, such as fish, poultry, beans, lentils, leafy greens, and fortified cereals. Recall that while non-heme iron **(derived from plants)** is less easily absorbed than heme iron **(found in animal sources)**, a combination of the two is preferable.

As the Conductor, Vitamin C This vitamin improves the absorption of nonheme iron by acting as a spotlight. Combine vitamin C-rich fruits and vegetables, such as tomatoes, bell peppers, and citrus fruits, with iron-rich plant-based foods. Imagine a spinach smoothie topped with berries or a lentil salad dressed with a zesty vinaigrette.

Add Some Flavor to the Absorption: Not only are black pepper and turmeric culinary heroes, but they're also backstage crew! The iron soloist can speak more clearly thanks to these spices, which increase iron solubility and bioavailability. For an added absorption boost, sprinkle them over your dishes that are high in iron.

Past the Plate:

Cooking Matters: Lower heat cooking techniques, such as grilling or frying, better retain iron content than gentle cooking techniques, such as steaming, simmering, and poaching. Reduce the amount of acidic ingredients in your cooking because they can bind to iron.

Soaking and Sprouting: Phytates, which are frequently found in grains and legumes, can prevent the absorption of iron. These foods can have their phytates reduced and iron bioavailability increased by soaking or sprouting.

Fermentation Magic: By making iron and other nutrients more readily available, fermented foods like kimchi and yogurt can improve the absorption of iron. Think about including them in your diet.

Hydration Harmony: Water is essential for the absorption of all nutrients, including iron. By staying well-hydrated throughout the day, you can optimize your body's absorption of iron.

Taking Care of Particular Issues:

Iron Warriors who are vegetarians and vegans: Although heme iron from animal sources is easily absorbed, a diet high in plants can still be high in iron! Prioritize a variety of plant-based sources, combine them with vitamin C, and, if necessary, take into account foods or supplements fortified with iron.

Crohn's and celiac disease champions: To manage your condition and maximize the absorption of iron, speak with your healthcare provider about specific dietary adjustments and options for iron supplementation.

Heavy Period Heroes: Menstrual iron losses can be substantial. Consult your physician about controlling your menstrual cycle and making sure you're getting enough iron from food or supplements.

Recall that treating issues with iron absorption is a customized process. Collaborate closely with your healthcare provider to pinpoint your unique requirements and create a customized strategy. Iron-rich symphonies of health can be created from your meals by adopting a varied and nutrient-dense diet, adding strategies to improve absorption, and getting medical advice when necessary. This will guarantee that your body gets the essential melody of health with every mouthful.

Bonus Advice: Never underestimate the value of relaxation and rest! Iron absorption can be adversely affected by stress. Make self-care a priority and control your stress levels to make sure your body is ready to absorb and use this vital mineral.

Now lift your fork, eat like a maestro, and unleash iron's full potential! You can experience the vibrant symphony of health that iron offers and overcome any absorption challenges with a little awareness, proactive effort, and support from your healthcare team.

○ Iron Symphony: Shutting Down the Blockers to Promote Optimal Absorption

Iron is your body's maestro of oxygen, so he deserves a quiet stage. However, unseen hindrances are waiting to muffle its essential melody. Iron warriors, do not be afraid! This guide will help you recognize and stop these absorption thieves so that your meals have a harmonious, iron-rich melody.

Comprehending the Reluctant Chorus:

Phytates: Iron's bioavailability can be decreased by these naturally occurring substances, which can be found in grains, legumes, and seeds. These foods can be made to soak, sprout, ferment, or cook in order to unlock the iron melody and dramatically lower phytate levels.

Although necessary for strong bones, calcium may face competition from iron in the absorption process. To prevent this competition, consume calcium-rich dairy products apart from meals high in iron.

Tea and coffee are popular drinks that include tannins that can bind to iron and prevent it from being absorbed. Reduce it, especially right before or right after iron-rich meals, or drink herbal teas instead.

Oxalic acid: This substance, which is present in rhubarb and spinach, has the ability to bind iron. Eat these foods in moderation along with sources of iron-rich foods, though they shouldn't be a big deal if you follow a balanced diet.

Fiber: Although necessary for gut health, too much fiber can hinder the absorption of iron. Prioritize soluble fiber sources such as fruits and vegetables and strive for a balanced intake.

Putting Your Meals in Harmony for Absorption:

Vitamin C, the Spotlight: This essential vitamin illuminates non-heme iron and improves its absorption by acting as a spotlight. Combine vitamin C-rich fruits and vegetables, such as tomatoes, bell peppers, and citrus fruits, with iron-rich plant-based foods. Imagine a spinach smoothie topped with berries or a lentil salad dressed with a zesty vinaigrette.

Spices, the crew backstage: Never undervalue the influence of spices! Black pepper and turmeric increase the bioavailability and solubility of iron, allowing the iron soloist to speak more clearly. For an added absorption boost, sprinkle them over your dishes that are high in iron.

Cooking Methods Are Important: Select low-heat cooking techniques such as poaching, steaming, and simmering over high-heat techniques like grilling or frying. These reduce the effects of inhibitors and maintain the iron content.

Acidic Balance: Since vinegar and lemon juice can bind with iron, stay away from them when cooking. Choose tomatoes and other acidic ingredients that are low in acidity, or dilute acidity by adding a small amount of baking soda.

Past the Plate:

Hydration Harmony: Water is essential for the absorption of all nutrients, including iron. Drink enough water throughout the day to keep your body functioning at its best for effective absorption of iron.

Why Gut Health Is Important An optimal gut microbiome can enhance the absorption of iron. Incorporate probiotics and prebiotics into your diet to help with nutrient absorption and gut health.

Pay Attention to Your Body: Observe your reactions to various foods and combinations. If you have any concerns regarding the absorption of iron, make the necessary adjustments to your meals and speak with a healthcare provider.

Meeting Particular Needs:

Iron Warriors who are vegetarians and vegans should emphasize a variety of plant-based iron sources, pair them with vitamin C, and, if necessary, look into iron-fortified foods or supplements.

Medical Conditions: Iron absorption may be impacted by specific medical conditions. Together with your medical provider, develop a diet and supplement plan that will help you manage your condition and absorb iron as efficiently as possible.

Recall that making thoughtful decisions rather than placing restrictions is what will silence the iron absorption inhibitors. Through comprehension of the functions of various inhibitors and integration of absorption-enhancing techniques into your dishes, you can convert your diet into an iron-dense orchestra, guaranteeing that your body gets the essential tune of well-being with each mouthwatering bite.

Bonus Tip: Remember the importance of preparation! Arranging your meals and snacks ahead of time will assist you in making wise decisions and warding off last-minute temptations that could impede the absorption of iron.

Raise your fork, eat like a maestro, and turn off the devices that prevent your body from absorbing iron! One delectable bite at a time, you can enjoy the vibrant symphony of health that iron offers with a little awareness, proactive effort, and a focus on nutrient synergy.

○ Getting Ahead in Nutrition: Handling Particular Dietary Requirements and Preferences

Food is what keeps our bodies going and keeps our souls full, but it can be difficult to navigate a world where there are so many different dietary requirements and preferences. Do not be alarmed, daring foodies! This guide serves as your compass, guiding you to a happy nutritional destination by helping you navigate a tasty path through a sea of constraints and desires.

Exposing the Dietary Needs Seafaring:

Allergies and Intolerances: These unexpected visitors may cause havoc with your digestive system. Nut-free, dairy-free, and gluten-free diet requirements can seem to go on forever. But do not worry! Accept the wide range of substitute ingredients, such as plant-based milks, nut-free butters, and gluten-free flours. Try new foods and uncover hidden treasures like cashew cheese that is creamy or pancakes made with chickpea flour.

Medical Conditions: Certain medical conditions call for particular dietary modifications. For instance, diabetics may need to choose their carbohydrates carefully. For individualized advice, speak with your healthcare provider. You can also try delectable options like lean protein sources, vegetables high in fiber, and fruits with low Glycemic index.

Ethical Decisions: The terms **"vegetarian,"** **"vegan,"** and **"pescatarian"** refer to various ethical perspectives on food. Salute the abundance of plant-based substitutes such as beans, lentils, tofu, and tempeh. Look into sustainable seafood sources and, if your path of choice permits, include dairy or eggs. Keep in mind that variety is essential, so heap a bright rainbow of delicious plant-based foods onto your plate.

Lifting the Preference Anchor:

Fans of flavor: Add some tangy sauces, strong herbs, and aromatic spices to your life. The world is your palate, from earthy turmeric to fiery chilis. Take risks and try new things to discover your ideal gastronomic balance.

Texture Templars: Do you yearn for the comforting creamy mashed potatoes or the crispiness of fresh vegetables? Knowing what textures you like best can help you choose foods. Savor hearty salads, light baked goods, or velvety soups; customize your meals to your favorite texture.

Time-Crunched Travelers: There may not be much time for elaborate culinary adventures due to life's hectic currents. Using canned or frozen foods, meal planning, and batch cooking can save your life. Accept easy and nutrient-dense options such as stir-fries, one-pan meals, and wholesome smoothies to stay satiated without compromising flavor or health.

Choosing a Balanced Path:

Nutritional Harmony: It's important to address individual needs and preferences, but it's also important to maintain a general nutritional balance. Aim for whole grains, lean protein sources, healthy fats, and a rainbow of fruits and vegetables. Enjoy all foods in their proper context and exercise mindful moderation rather than demonizing any particular food group.

Pay Attention to Your Body: It serves as a compass and will whisper to you what nutrients it needs. Take note of your feelings after eating various foods. Give top priority to foods that give you energy and steer clear of those that make you feel uneasy or lethargic.

Accept the Journey: Maintaining dietary requirements and preferences calls for ongoing investigation rather than a straight path.

Celebrate your accomplishments, have patience with yourself, and don't be afraid to change direction when necessary. Keep in mind that the most crucial component is enjoyment, so relish each bite and sail through your dietary challenges with joy!

Bonus Advice: Recall that eating is a social activity! Create enduring memories around the table, explore new cuisines with those you love, and share your culinary adventures with them. We can all gracefully and joyfully navigate the varied waters of dietary needs and preferences if we help one another and cultivate an inclusive spirit.

Now lift your fork, embark on your gastronomic adventure, and explore the countless options that lie ahead! One bite at a time, you can steer toward a tasty and nourishing life with a little forethought, ingenuity, and self-compassion.

○ **Getting Through the Nutritional Maze: Knowing When to Get Expert Advice for Tailored Solutions**

Trying to make sense of the complex world of nutrition can be like navigating a maze. You may feel lost and confused due to the abundance of dietary theories, contradicting information, and constantly shifting goals. But brave adventurers, do not be alarmed! Seeking professional advice can often be the most empowering move because it can open the door to individualized solutions and provide a clear route towards achieving optimal health.

When to Look for the Expert Lighthouse:

Chronic Health Conditions: Dietary modifications are frequently necessary for people who live with conditions such as diabetes, celiac disease, or autoimmune disorders. Getting advice from a qualified nutritionist or dietitian can be extremely helpful in creating a safe and sensible eating schedule that will control your symptoms and enhance your overall health.

Progress Has Plateaued: Struggling to meet certain fitness objectives or caught in a weight reduction rut? A specialist can assist in locating nutritional obstacles, modify your caloric intake and the ratio of macronutrients, and provide tailored strategies to help you overcome plateaus and reach your goals.

Complex Dietary Needs: It can be quite difficult to manage several dietary restrictions or complicated medical conditions. In addition to making sure you meet all of your nutritional needs, a registered dietitian can offer professional advice on how to manage food allergies, intolerances, and moral decisions.

Overwhelmed by confusing information: Lost in a sea of contradictory dietary recommendations and fashions? A specialist can assist you in sorting through the confusion, dispelling myths, and converting scientific findings into useful, doable actions that suit your particular requirements and preferences.

Motivation and Accountability: Do you require an extra push to complete your tasks on time? As your cheerleader, a registered dietitian or nutritionist can offer you continuous accountability, inspiration, and support to help you stick to your objectives and recognize your accomplishments along the way.

Locating Your North Star in Nutrition:

Qualifications and Credentials: Seek out licensed nutritionists or registered dietitians **(RDs)** with experience in fields related to your needs and with credentials that are acknowledged.

Communication and Approach: Pick a specialist who pays close attention to your worries, is cognizant of your way of life, and uses clear, relatable language when communicating.

Tailored Approaches and Plans: Steer clear of formulaic approaches! Seek experts who can create personalized plans based on your particular requirements, preferences, and health issues.

Collaboration: Never forget that you are a team! Select a provider who will actively involve you in creating and carrying out your customized nutrition plan and who values your opinions.

Constant Assistance and Flexibility: Eating well is a lifelong process. Seek out experts who provide continuing assistance, make necessary adjustments to your plan, and acknowledge your accomplishments at every stage.

Outside the Consultation Room

Accept Self-Education: Although expert advice is priceless, arm yourself with knowledge!

Engage in workshops, read reliable nutrition sources, and pose knowledgeable queries to take an active role in your own health journey.

Try New Things and Adapt: Don't be scared to take risks and modify your plan in light of your findings. Pay attention to what your body tells you, figure out what foods suit you best, and accept that your nutritional needs are always changing.

Enjoy the Journey: Keep in mind that development takes time! Celebrate the little victories in life, give yourself credit for your work, and take pleasure in the process of figuring out what genuinely fuels your body and mind.

Seeking expert advice for customized solutions is an act of empowerment rather than weakness. With the guidance of a trained expert, you can successfully negotiate the nutritional maze and gain access to individualized tactics, continuous inspiration, and a direct route to your ideal state of health and wellbeing. Now take a deep breath, plot your course, and approach the lighthouse of professional competence with assurance. A path to a more vibrant and healthy version of yourself is waiting for you!

Bonus Advice: Remember the influence of your community! Create a network of mutual growth and encouragement by connecting with people who share your nutritional goals and challenges, finding inspiration and support, and sharing your own experiences.

Recall that navigating the world of nutrition is an ongoing journey. Accept the path, acknowledge the little victories, and have faith in the procedure. One delicious bite at a time, you can discover the secrets of your individual nutritional needs and set out on a path to a healthier and more satisfying life with the help of a supportive community, self-education, and professional guidance!

Part 4:

Beyond Diet: A Comprehensive Strategy to Realize the Full Potential of Iron

Within our bodies, iron, the blood that keeps our cells alive, dances a delicate waltz. It emotes our blood a deep crimson, powers our muscles to move with force, and composes the energy production symphony. However, this essential mineral may turn into a muted melody for a lot of people, its bright notes hidden in the darkness of deficiency. Unlocking the full potential of iron requires a holistic approach, a symphony of factors that work together to nourish our bodies and minds, even though dietary choices play a crucial role in iron health.

Beyond the Plate: Iron Health's Supporting Cast

Sleep, the Restorative Conductor: Our bodies renew and repair themselves while we sleep, and iron is essential to this nighttime activity. Adults need 7-8 hours of sleep per night in order to produce the hormone hepcidin, which controls the absorption of iron. Hepcidin levels can increase in response to sleep disturbances, which can impair iron absorption and leave you feeling exhausted.

Exercise and Its Energizing Companion: Movement is like a bright light, directing iron toward muscles that are in need of oxygen. Frequent exercise, even if it's just gentle yoga or moderate walks, improves iron utilization and red blood cell production, which will increase your energy and general wellbeing.

Stress, the Disharmonious Chorus: Prolonged stress can resemble an unbalanced note in an iron-string orchestra. Fatigue and a compromised immune system can result from iron absorption and utilization being disrupted by the stress hormone cortisol. To maintain iron's harmonious flow, learn to manage stress through mindfulness exercises, deep breathing techniques, or time spent outdoors.

Gut Consistency, the Fundamental Basis: For the absorption of iron, a healthy gut microbiome is similar to fertile soil. Fermented foods, as well as some fruits and vegetables, contain probiotics and prebiotics, which are good bacteria that aid in the absorption of iron and aid in digestion. To ensure the best possible absorption of iron, nourish your stomach.

Adjusting Your Lifestyle for Iron Harmony:

The Life-Giving Stream: Hydration Water maintains the seamless flow of the iron symphony. Eight glasses of water a day should be the goal in order to guarantee sufficient blood volume and good nutrient transport, which will enable iron to get to its destination effectively.

The Spotlight Conductor, Vitamin C: This bright vitamin illuminates non-heme iron and increases its absorption like a spotlight. Combine vitamin C-rich fruits and vegetables, such as citrus fruits, bell peppers, and tomatoes, with iron-rich plant sources, such as lentils, beans, and leafy greens.

Taking Care When Cooking: Steaming, simmering, and poaching are examples of gentle cooking techniques that maintain iron content and stop it from evaporating into cooking liquid. Steer clear of high-heat cooking techniques like frying and grilling as these can harm the fragile iron molecule.

Iron-Rigged Options: Think about foods like bread, milk, and cereals that have been fortified with iron, particularly if you have trouble getting enough iron from your diet. If necessary, discuss appropriate iron supplements with your healthcare provider.

Recall that iron health is a dynamic ensemble rather than a solo act. These all-encompassing techniques combined with a conscious and well-balanced diet can turn your body into a platform where iron's essential melody is felt in every movement, breath, and heartbeat. Experience the full, harmonious glory of iron's transformative power by paying attention to your body and tending to its needs.

Bonus Advice: Never undervalue the importance of self-compassion! On your path to iron health, treat yourself with kindness. Honor your accomplishments, take lessons from failures, and never forget that progress is a journey, not a destination.

One tasty bite, mindful movement, and peaceful night at a time, embrace the holistic symphony of iron health and watch your body blossom with vibrant energy, strength, and well-being!

Chapter 11:

The Power Chord: Sleep and Exercise Balanced for Best Health

Consider your body as a dynamic symphony, with every system acting as an instrument to contribute to the overall composition of health. Exercise and sleep are two crucial, but frequently underappreciated, instruments in this orchestra. These two power chords work together to produce a symphony of well-being that enhances vitality, immunity, and energy levels.

The Energizing Maestro Exercise:

Exercise is a powerful conductor of health benefits, extending beyond toned bodies and sculpted muscles. Frequent exercise, even mild exercise like dancing or brisk walks, has many positive effects on your body and mind.

Boosts Energy and Mood: Engaging in physical activity causes the body to release endorphins, which are feel-good, stress-relieving chemicals. This translates into more vitality, less exhaustion, and a happier perspective on life. Builds and maintains muscle mass, which enhances strength, flexibility, and balance. Strengthens Muscles and Bones. Moreover, it fortifies bones, lowering the chance of fractures and osteoporosis.

Enhances Cardiovascular Health: Exercise reduces the risk of heart disease and stroke by strengthening your heart and lungs, which improves blood flow and oxygen delivery to cells.

Controls Metabolism and Weight: Exercise burns calories and aids in maintaining a healthy weight. Additionally, it raises your metabolic rate, which enables your body to burn more calories while at rest and throughout the day.

The Restorative Symphony that is sleep:

Exercise gives you energy, but sleep is the restorative conductor that lets your body and mind recuperate.

A series of essential functions take place while you sleep:

Cellular Repair and Regeneration: Hormones that repair and regenerate cells in your body, including your muscles, tissues, and brain, are released when you sleep. The preservation of both physical and mental health depends on this process.

Learning and Memory Consolidation: Learning and memory consolidation depend on sleep. Your brain consolidates new knowledge and skills acquired during the day by processing and storing it during sleep.

Immune System Boost: Getting enough sleep fortifies your immune system, increasing your resistance to diseases and infections. Getting enough sleep aids in the body's production of antibodies and defense cells that fend against illness.

Stress Reduction and Emotional Control: Getting enough sleep aids in stress management and emotional control. Your body releases hormones while you sleep that work against stress hormones to encourage emotional stability and relaxation.

The Harmonious Duet

The benefits of exercise and sleep are multiplied when they are combined, resulting in a potent synergy for optimal health:

Exercise Promotes Deeper Sleep Stages and Reduces Nighttime Disruptions: Engaging in regular physical activity can enhance sleep quality. Exercise causes physical exhaustion, which facilitates falling and staying asleep.

Sleep Enhances Exercise Performance: Getting enough sleep prepares your body and mind for the best possible workout. It increases endurance and coordination, lessens the chance of injury, and speeds up muscle recovery.

They Fight Chronic Illnesses Together: For the purpose of managing and preventing chronic illnesses like obesity, diabetes, and heart disease, exercise and sleep are essential. The lifespan is increased and general well-being is enhanced by this synergistic effect.

Harmonizing Your Orchestra:

To reach their maximum potential, finding the ideal balance between exercise and sleep is essential. Try to get in at least 150 minutes a week of moderate-to-intense exercise, broken down into shorter sessions if necessary. Make it a priority to get 7-8 hours of good sleep every night. You can also practice relaxation techniques before bed and create a regular sleep schedule.

Recall that you are not performing alone in the symphony of health. Seek assistance from close friends and family, medical professionals, and wellness groups to establish a long-term lifestyle that places equal importance on exercise and rest. One energizing workout and restful night at a time, you can experience the vibrant melody of optimal health by listening to your body, honoring its needs, and nurturing the harmonious duet of exercise and sleep.

Bonus Advice: Remember the importance of mindfulness! Include techniques like deep breathing or meditation in your routine to help you sleep better and manage stress. You can cultivate a favorable environment for mental and physical health by stilling the mind.

Thus, increase your heart rate through exercise and welcome sleep's restorative embrace. Allow these two powerful chords to harmonize, and observe as your health develops into a lively, resilient, and joyful symphony!

○ **Iron Symphony: The Primary Role That Exercise Plays in Absorption**

Your cells' oxygen conductor, iron, longs for a platform on which to play its essential tune. However, poor absorption pushes this important mineral to the background for some people. Come on, exercise, the dynamic choreographer, prepared to put iron absorption front and center and create a colorful health symphony.

The Way Iron and Movement Interact:

Exercise affects iron absorption in a variety of intriguing ways and isn't just about toned bodies and sculpted muscles:

Boosts Blood Flow: Movement improves blood circulation, which makes it easier for tissues to receive oxygen- and iron-rich red blood cells. This better delivery system means that iron is absorbed from food sources more effectively.

Exercise promotes muscle repair, which raises the need for iron to make hemoglobin and myoglobin, the proteins in red blood cells and muscle tissue that carry oxygen. This increased need functions as a spotlight, increasing the amount of iron in your diet and improving its absorption.

Hepcidin, the Iron Gatekeeper: Hepcidin is a hormone that controls the absorption of iron, and exercise can lower hepcidin levels. The gates spread apart when hepcidin levels are reduced, letting more dietary iron enter your circulation and be used by your cells.

Spontaneous Combustion: Excessive-intensity exercise can microbleed muscles, allowing the blood to carry stored iron. Even though it might seem strange at first, this gives your body a brief boost in iron availability so that it has enough for your immediate needs.

Bringing the Iron Symphony and Movement into Harmony:

Exercise is the conductor, but a number of other elements also contribute to the best possible iron absorption:

Timing of Performance: Avoid intense physical activity immediately before or after meals high in iron as this may impair absorption. To maximize effectiveness, wait at least two hours between exercising and iron-rich foods.

The Spotlight Conductor, Vitamin C: This colorful vitamin helps absorb non-heme iron, which is mostly found in plant-based sources. Combine vitamin C-rich fruits and vegetables, such as tomatoes, bell peppers, and citrus fruits, with iron-rich plant foods.

Modest Cooking: Cooking techniques that use high heat can corrode iron, decreasing its bioavailability. Choose gentler techniques to maximize absorption and maintain iron content, such as poaching, simmering, or steaming.

Pay Attention to Your Body: Keep an eye on how your iron levels are impacted by various forms and levels of exercise. If you notice any symptoms of an iron deficiency, modify your routine accordingly and see a doctor.

Beyond the Stage:

Exercise is important, but keep in mind that iron absorption is a complicated dance involving numerous partners:

Make a variety of iron-rich plant and animal-based food choices as a top priority in your diet. Add legumes, beans, fish, poultry, red meat, and leafy greens to your diet.

Gut Health: Iron absorption is supported by a healthy gut microbiome. Consume foods high in probiotics and prebiotics, such as fruits, vegetables, kefir, yogurt, and fermented vegetables.

Sufficient Hydration: Water helps your body absorb iron. Eight glasses of water a day should be the goal for best absorption and utilization.

Control Stress: Prolonged stress can hinder the absorption of iron. To reduce stress and promote general well being, try relaxation methods like yoga, meditation, or deep breathing.

Recall that the iron symphony is a group endeavor rather than a solo performance. You can shift your body into a state where iron absorption thrives by combining these supportive strategies with consistent exercise. As you pay attention to your body, make iron-rich food choices, move mindfully, and listen to its needs, you'll see a blossoming of vibrant energy, strength, and well-being in your health.

Bonus Advice: Never undervalue the influence of a community! Seek out exercise partners or enroll in groups to receive encouragement and support. You can increase the enjoyment and sustainability of the journey by sharing your iron symphony with others.

One energizing workout and mouth watering bite at a time, embrace the dynamic interaction between physical activity and iron absorption, and feel the transformative power of movement as it guides your body towards optimal iron health!

○ **Rest, the Calm Conductor: Harmonizing Iron's Vital Notes**

Iron, the conductor of oxygen in our cells, needs a bright stage in order to thrive. However, due to inadequate absorption and utilization, this important mineral is often overlooked. But do not worry! Sleep is the calm conductor who is about to set the stage for a symphony of iron metabolism in your body, allowing this essential component to sing its full and vibrant melody.

The Relationship Between Iron and Sleep:

As night falls and we begin to sleep, an intriguing interaction between iron and sleep occurs:

Hepcidin's Harmonic Hibernation: Hepcidin is a hormone that controls the absorption of iron. Its levels naturally decrease while you sleep. Because of this dip, which functions as a lowered curtain, more iron from your diet and stored reserves can enter your bloodstream.

Sleep is a time for cellular regeneration and repair, as well as for the replenishment of iron stores. Iron is further utilized in this process because it is needed for the synthesis of new tissues, proteins, and enzymes.

Metabolic Maestro: Iron homeostasis is one of the metabolic processes that sleep controls. This guarantees the effective use of iron that has been absorbed, avoiding imbalances and fostering optimal function.

The Immune Symphony: Getting enough sleep fortifies your immune system, which is largely dependent on iron to function. This strengthened immune system aids in the fight against infections and inflammatory conditions that can impede the uptake and utilization of iron.

Balancing the Iron Symphony and Sleep:

Try to maintain a healthy sleep schedule in order to optimize the benefits of sleep on iron metabolism:

Make Quality Sleep a Priority: Try to get between seven and eight hours of sleep every night. To encourage deeper sleep, set up a soothing bedtime routine and stick to a regular sleep schedule.

Pay Attention to Your Meals: A large meal right before bed can interfere with sleep and reduce the absorption of iron. Instead, choose lighter, more easily absorbed snacks.

Light and Darkness: Reduce your exposure to light right before bed to create a sleep-friendly atmosphere. Reduce the lights and use blackout curtains to let your body know when it's time to relax.

Control Your Stress: Prolonged stress can harm iron metabolism and interfere with sleep. Utilize relaxation methods to control stress and encourage restful sleep, such as yoga, deep breathing, or meditation.

Past the Stage of Slumber:

Although sleep is important, keep in mind that iron metabolism is a complicated dance with other important partners:

Make a variety of iron-rich food choices, such as red meat, chicken, fish, beans, lentils, and leafy greens, a priority in your diet. To improve the absorption of nonheme iron, combine these with fruits and vegetables that are high in vitamin C. Physical Activity: Iron absorption and utilization are aided by regular exercise, which increases blood flow and oxygen delivery. Try to get in at least 150 minutes a week of moderate-to-intense exercise.

Stay hydrated: Water helps your body carry iron throughout your body. Throughout the day, sip on lots of water to guarantee optimal absorption and utilization.

Handle Medical Conditions: Iron metabolism may be impacted by specific medical conditions. If you have any questions or long-term health conditions that may affect how well you absorb or use iron, speak with your doctor.

Recall that the iron symphony is a group endeavor rather than a solo performance. If you combine these supportive strategies with a healthy sleep schedule, you can shift your body into a state where iron metabolism thrives. Pay attention to what your body needs, give it iron-rich foods, make restful sleep a priority, and watch as your health blossoms with vibrant energy, strength, and overall well-being.

Bonus Advice: The importance of routine cannot be overstated! Establish a regular sleep schedule and try your best to maintain it, even on the weekends. This optimizes the benefits for your iron metabolism by promoting deeper sleep and assisting in the regulation of your body's natural sleep-wake cycle.

Accept the peaceful melody of sleep and its essential function in the metabolism of iron. Let your body compose the iron symphony as you drift off to sleep, and when you awaken, you'll feel a lively chorus of health resonating within you.

○ Putting Fuel into Your Iron Symphony: A Handbook for Creating a Dynamic Lifestyle

Iron, the conductor of oxygen in your cells, longs for a lively platform to play its vital note. However, this essential mineral is often overlooked due to insufficiency. Do not be alarmed! You can give iron the ideal environment to grow and empower your body with a symphony of health by leading a healthy lifestyle.

The Dynamic Ensemble of Iron Health:

Think of your body as a large orchestra, with every instrument contributing to the harmonious whole of iron health.

The following are the main instruments:

Dietary Harmony: Give different foods high in iron, derived from plants and animals, priority. Accept lentils, fish, poultry, beans, leafy greens, and red meat. Remember vitamin C, the star conductor, to improve the absorption of nonheme iron! Bell peppers, tomatoes, and citrus fruits go well with plant foods high in iron.

The Dynamic Choreographer of Movement: Exercise is a choreographer of iron absorption, not just for toned muscles! Try to get in at least 150 minutes a week of moderate-to-intense exercise. Increased blood flow, a higher demand for iron in muscles, and a decrease in hepcidin—the iron gatekeeper—allow for better absorption.

The Calm Conductor, Sleep: Sleep is a master of iron metabolism, not just a place to rest! Hepcidin levels fall when we sleep, which makes more iron available for absorption into the blood. Furthermore, sleep promotes cellular repair by requiring and utilizing iron for the regeneration of tissue. Aim for seven to eight hours of good sleep every night.

The Life-Giving Stream: Hydration Water is a vital component for all biological functions, including the transportation of iron. Eight glasses of water a day should be the goal for best absorption and utilization.

Stress Reduction, the Balancing Power: Iron absorption and utilization are disrupted by ongoing stress. Use relaxation methods to control your stress and maintain the harmony of your iron symphony, such as yoga, meditation, or deep breathing.

How to Make Your Own Iron Symphony:

Recall that there isn't a single iron health strategy that works for everyone.

Here's how to make your orchestra uniquely yours:

Listen to Your Body: Observe how your energy levels and iron status are affected by various foods, activities, and sleep schedules. Adapt your lifestyle accordingly, seeking medical advice from a professional if necessary.

Accept Diverse Rhythms: Stay out of a rut! Change up your workout regimens, try new foods, and give priority to things you enjoy doing. This maintains the vibrancy and interest of your iron symphony.

Seek Harmony and Support: Those who celebrate your accomplishments and promote healthy habits should be your circle of support. If you need inspiration and motivation, think about signing up for cooking classes or fitness groups.

Honor Minor Victories: Do not wait for significant accomplishments! Celebrate and give thanks for each step you take in the direction of a healthy lifestyle. This encouragement feeds your iron symphony and keeps you driven.

Past the Stage: A Comprehensive Method:

Recall that iron health encompasses more than just what occurs in the gym or on the plate.

Think about these components of the holistic approach:

Gut Health Is Important: Iron absorption is aided by a healthy gut microbiome. Consume foods high in probiotics and prebiotics, such as fermented vegetables, kefir, and yogurt.

Handle Medical Conditions: Iron absorption may be impacted by specific medical conditions. If you have any concerns, seek individual advice from your healthcare provider.

Mindful Eating: Enjoy your food and keep your mind off other things. This encourages improved nutrient absorption, including iron absorption, and digestion.

Joy and Connection: Engage in things that make you happy and foster relationships with other people. Your overall health, including the absorption of iron, can be positively impacted by laughter, social interaction, and a sense of purpose.

Putting Your Iron Symphony to Work:

Establishing a healthy lifestyle for ideal iron levels is a dynamic, continuous process rather than a quick fix. You can change your body into a stage where iron flourishes by implementing these techniques, paying attention to your body, and appreciating each step. Accept the harmony of iron health and feel the delight of being robust, energized, and prepared to face each day with a smile!

Recall that your well-being is your masterpiece. Now grab your instruments, hone your skills, and produce the liveliest iron symphony your body can produce!

Chapter 12:

Getting Through the Iron Labyrinth: When and How to Take Supplemental Information

Iron, the element that gives our cells life, oxygenates our tissues, gives our blood its vivid red color, and powers our energy. However, this necessary mineral can become a whisper rather than a roar for many people, leaving them feeling exhausted and depleted. Although dietary decisions are frequently the main factor affecting iron health, supplements occasionally take center stage and give a supporting performance. However, figuring out the maze of iron supplements can be challenging. Do not be alarmed, my fellow travelers! With the information in this guide, you'll be able to confidently choose when and how to approach these formidable allies.

Knowing When to Get Iron Support

It's important to determine whether supplements are actually necessary before reaching for them.

In the event that you encounter any of the following indicators of iron deficiency, speak with your doctor:

Fatigue and low energy: Constantly feeling exhausted, even after getting enough sleep, may indicate an iron deficiency.

Pale lips, skin, and mucous membranes: The color-giving qualities of iron can be lost, resulting in pale lips, skin, and inner eyelids.

Iron is essential for healthy hair and nails, especially in cases of brittle nails. Their susceptibility to breakage may indicate a deficit. Breathlessness and lightheadedness: Low iron levels can affect the way oxygen is delivered, which can cause dyspnea and vertigo, particularly when exercising.

Excessive or irregular menstrual bleeding: Because of blood loss, women who experience heavy or irregular periods are more likely to experience iron deficiency.

The Variable Cast of Iron Amalgamations

Not every supplement containing iron is made equal!

Knowing how they differ will help you make wise decisions:

Non-ferrous vs. Ferrous: In general, ferrous iron absorbs more readily than non-ferrous forms. Ferrous fumarate, ferrous gluconate, and ferrous sulfate are examples of common ferrous options.

Dosage Considerations: The suggested daily dosage is based on the severity of your deficiency and your unique needs. See your healthcare provider for individual advice.

Form and Delivery: There are several ways to take iron supplements, such as tablets, capsules, liquids, and injectables. Every form has a different rate of absorption and possible adverse effects.

Improving the Harmony of Your Iron Supplements:

Use these practical recommendations to optimize the advantages and reduce any potential drawbacks of iron supplements:

Collaborate with Food: Consuming iron can be improved by eating foods high in vitamin C, such as tomatoes, bell peppers, and citrus fruits. Steer clear of coffee and dairy products right before consumption as they may interfere with absorption.

Consider the Timing: If meals upset your stomach, take your dosage after other activities. Try a variety of times of day to see what suits you the best.

Kind to the Gut: Select mild formulations, particularly if your digestion is delicate. As tolerated, progressively increase dosage from lower starting points.

Drinking Water Harmony: To help with absorption and avoid constipation, which is a common side effect of iron supplements, sip lots of water throughout the day.

Listen to Your Body: After taking iron supplements, observe your body's reaction. See your doctor for more options or dosage adjustments if you encounter any unpleasant side effects, such as nausea, constipation, or diarrhea.

Past the Stage of Supplementation Information:

Recall that iron supplements are not a panacea. To maximize your iron health, they should be used in conjunction with a well-balanced diet full of foods high in iron, enough sleep, and frequent physical activity. For advice on dietary changes, exercise regimens, and possible underlying causes of your iron deficiency, speak with your healthcare provider.

The Iron Curtain's closure:

Understanding the maze of iron supplements, working with others, and having a dedication to your health are necessary for success. Iron can become a vibrant roar, giving your body the energy and vitality it deserves, by helping you understand your needs, selecting the right supplements, and working with your healthcare provider. Recall that you are in charge of your own health symphony, and one of the most important instruments in your orchestra is iron. Thus, assume the initiative, pay attention to your body, and create a masterpiece of iron-health!

- **Getting Through the Iron Maze: When to Think About Supplementing**

Within us, iron plays a vibrant symphony of energy and vitality. Iron is the maestro of oxygen in our cells. However, this necessary mineral can become a muted melody for many people, leaving them feeling exhausted. Although dietary decisions are frequently the primary factor in iron health, supplements occasionally take center stage. It can be difficult to know when to call upon these powerful allies, but fear not! You will gain the knowledge from this guide to be able to determine whether iron supplementation is necessary with confidence.

Detecting the Whisper of Your Body:

Knowing whether your body is really in need of supplements before taking them is important.

Keep an eye out for these subliminal cues that your body may be sending:

Fatigue and Low Energy: Constantly feeling exhausted, even after getting enough sleep, may indicate an iron deficiency. Your everyday activities may be hampered by this ongoing fatigue, which can also make you feel unusually lethargic.

Pale Skin and Mucous Membranes: Pale lips, inner eyelids, and skin can all be signs of the color-giving properties of iron being lost. This paleness may be an obvious sign that you are low on iron supplies.

Iron is essential for healthy and strong hair and nails, especially if you have brittle nails and hair. Their brittleness, which manifests as severe hair loss or cracked nails, may indicate an iron deficiency.

Breathlessness and Lightheadedness: Low iron levels can affect the way oxygen is delivered, which can cause dyspnea and vertigo, particularly when exercising. These signs are concerning and need to be taken seriously.

Heavy or Irregular Menstrual Bleeding: Because of blood loss, women who experience heavy or irregular periods are more likely to experience iron deficiency. This may worsen existing symptoms such as exhaustion and lead to iron deficiency.

Seeking Advice from the Specialist:

Even though these whispers can be a useful place to start, it's imperative that you seek medical advice. They will accurately measure your iron levels and identify any underlying conditions that may be causing the deficiency through a comprehensive evaluation that includes blood tests.

The Variable Cast of Iron Amalgamations

Not every supplement containing iron is made equal!

Comprehending their distinctions is essential to jointly making knowledgeable decisions with your healthcare provider:

Non-ferrous vs. Ferrous: In general, the body absorbs ferrous iron more readily than non-ferrous forms. Ferrous fumarate, ferrous gluconate, and ferrous sulfate are examples of common ferrous options.

Dosage Considerations: The suggested daily dosage is based on the severity of your deficiency and your unique needs. The dosage will be customized by your healthcare provider for your unique circumstances.

Structure and Distribution: There are several different types of iron supplements, such as tablets, capsules, liquids, and injectables. Every form has a different rate of absorption and possible adverse effects. Your doctor will advise you on the best form based on your requirements and preferences.

Iron Health's Harmonious Symphony:

Recall that taking iron supplements is a team effort. They ought to be taken in conjunction with a well-balanced diet full of foods high in iron, such as fish, poultry, red meat, beans, lentils, and leafy greens. In addition, getting enough sleep, exercising frequently, and controlling your stress are all essential for maintaining optimal iron health.

The Iron Curtain's closure:

Determining if you need iron supplements is a delicate dance between self-awareness, expert advice, and a dedication to holistic health. You can change the dull melody of iron deficiency into a vibrant symphony of energy, vitality, and well-being by paying attention to your body's whispers, seeing a healthcare provider, and making educated supplement decisions. Recall that you are the leader of your own health orchestra, and one of the most important instruments in your toolkit is iron. Thus, assume the initiative, pay attention to your body's cues, and create a masterpiece of iron health!

- **Getting Through the Iron Maze: Selecting the Best Supplement for Your Requirements**

Your cells' oxygen conductor, iron, creates a colorful symphony of vitality and wellbeing. However, it occasionally requires assistance, just like any conductor. Supplemental iron can act as those helpful musicians, stepping in to raise your blood iron levels and help your body reach its optimal, harmonious state. Choosing the appropriate supplement, however, can feel like navigating a bewildering musical score because there are so many options available. Do not be alarmed, musicians who are concerned about their health! With the information in this guide, you will be able to choose the best performer for your particular needs and confidently navigate the confusing world of iron supplements.

Getting in Tune with Your Body's Tone:

It's important to recognize the specific composition and iron requirements of your body before reaching for supplements. For a comprehensive assessment, speak with your healthcare provider, who serves as the conductor of your health orchestra. Your blood work will be examined, possible underlying conditions will be evaluated, and the actual cause of your iron deficiency will be determined. This individualized approach guarantees that you select the appropriate supplement rather than just any old device from the health store.

The Varying Cast of Iron Tools:

Similar to how different instruments produce distinct tones, there are several forms of iron supplements, each with advantages and disadvantages of its own:

Non-Ferrous vs. Ferrous: Consider ferrous iron to be the main act, as it is typically more readily absorbed than non-ferrous alternatives. Ferrous fumarate, ferrous gluconate, and ferrous sulfate are examples of common ferrous players.

Dosage Considerations: The suggested daily dosage directs you toward the best outcomes, much like a music sheet. To make sure you don't overplay or underperform, your healthcare provider will customize the dosage to meet your unique needs.

Structure and Distribution: Each type of iron supplement—tablets, capsules, liquids, and injectables—is like a different tool, with distinct benefits and possible drawbacks. Find the form that best suits your needs by talking to your healthcare provider about your preferences and sensitivity levels.

Enhancing the Iron Symphony:

Recall that supplements are merely one piece in the whole health orchestra.

Take into consideration these supporting acts to truly harmonize your iron levels:

Dietary Harmony: Provide your body with iron-rich foods such as leafy greens, beans, lentils, chicken, and red meat. These organic sources offer iron in a variety of forms, enhancing the overall harmony of your health.

The dynamic choreographer movement: Exercise increases the body's ability to absorb and use iron. To keep your iron symphony in motion, try to get in at least 150 minutes of moderate-intensity exercise each week.

The Calm Conductor, Sleep: A healthy sleep schedule enables your body to recycle and repair iron. Try to get 7–8 hours of good sleep every night to reward your iron metabolism with a little extra.

Paying Attention to Your Body's Input:

As with any skilled musician, observe your body's reaction to the new iron supplement. Common adverse effects include constipation and mild nausea, which are usually temporary and controllable. However, you should contact your healthcare provider right away if you feel excruciating or persistent discomfort. They can suggest different forms, change the dosage, or find any underlying sensitivities that could be the source of the dissonance.

The Iron Curtain's closure:

Selecting the appropriate iron supplement requires cooperation from your body, your healthcare provider, and yourself. You can change the muted melody of iron deficiency into a vibrant symphony of energy, vitality, and well-being by paying attention to your needs, comprehending the range of options, and placing a high priority on a holistic approach to iron health. Recall that iron is a crucial instrument in your musical journey, and that you are the conductor of your own health orchestra. Thus, assume the initiative, pay attention to your body's signals, and create a masterpiece of iron health!

And never forget that maintaining your health is not a sport. Concentrate on balancing your own iron symphony and allow the distinct melody of your body to come through!

    ○ **Getting Around the Iron Labyrinth: A Handbook for Safe and Efficient Iron Intake**

The red color of blood and the source of our energy, iron, is like a dynamic conductor directing an orchestra. Iron is the lifeblood of our cells. However, occasionally this necessary mineral can become a muted melody, leaving us feeling exhausted. Although iron supplements can be powerful allies, it's important to know their limitations and potential in order to use them safely and effectively. So let's set out on a voyage through the iron labyrinth, equipped with the knowledge and ability to make decisions that will lead to our best health.

Prior to the First Note:

Be mindful that supplements are not a one-size-fits-all remedy before reaching for them. Speak with your healthcare provider—the conductor of your health. They will check your iron levels, look for any underlying issues, and recommend the best course of action. This individualized approach guarantees that you don't use a deafening dose of supplements to treat a whisper of a deficiency.

Exposing the Varied Spectrum of Iron Supplements:

There are several types of iron supplements, and each has advantages and disadvantages of its own:

Non-Ferrous vs. Ferrous: Consider ferrous iron to be the main act, as it is typically more readily absorbed than non-ferrous alternatives. Ferrous fumarate, ferrous gluconate, and ferrous sulfate are examples of common ferrous players.

Dosage Considerations: The suggested daily dosage acts as a safe and reliable guide, much like a music sheet. Your doctor will adjust the dosage based on your individual needs to prevent potentially dangerous overdosing.

Structure and Distribution: Each form of the drug—tablets, capsules, liquids, and injectables—is like a different tool, with unique benefits and possible drawbacks. Together with your healthcare provider, go over your preferences and sensitivities to determine which form best suits your needs and reduces any potential discomfort.

Syncing with the Rhythm of Your Body:

Supplements are only one piece in the whole orchestra of health.

Take into account these supporting actions to genuinely maximize your iron levels:

Dietary Harmony: Provide your body with iron-rich foods such as leafy greens, beans, lentils, chicken, and red meat. These organic sources offer iron in a variety of forms, enhancing your body's symphony of health without the possible negative effects of supplements.

The dynamic choreographer movement: Exercise increases the body's ability to absorb and use iron. To keep your iron symphony in motion, try to get in at least 150 minutes of moderate-intensity exercise each week.

The Calm Conductor, Sleep: Your body is able to repair and regulate iron levels when you get enough sleep. For the best possible rest and optimization of your iron metabolism, try to get 7-8 hours of good sleep every night.

Paying Attention to Your Body's Input:

As with any skilled musician, observe your body's reaction to the new iron supplement. Common adverse effects include constipation and mild nausea, which are usually temporary and controllable. But if you encounter severe, enduring, or worrisome side effects, get in touch with your doctor right away. They can suggest different forms, change the dosage, or find any underlying sensitivities that could be the source of the conflict.

The Iron Curtain's closure:

Using iron supplements safely requires cooperation and knowledge. You can turn the dull melody of iron deficiency into a vibrant symphony of energy, vitality, and well-being by emphasizing a holistic approach to iron health, paying close attention to your body's feedback, and collaborating closely with your healthcare provider. Recall that iron is a crucial instrument in your musical journey, and that you are the conductor of your own health orchestra. Thus, assume the initiative, pay attention to the rhythms and whispers of your body, and create a masterpiece of iron health!

Together, let's embrace the distinctive melody of your health and compose a beautiful symphony of wellbeing for all!

Chapter 13:

From Seed to Concerto: Unveiling the Potential of Iron from Plants

Our every movement and thought is powered by iron, the maestro of oxygen in our cells, who conducts a vibrant symphony of energy. Although a lot of people think that red meat is the source of iron, there are a ton of potential plant-based options that are just waiting to be discovered. So, give up on dietary restrictions and welcome the world of plant-based iron choices that are empowering!

Beyond Beef: An Assorted Cast of Plants High in Iron

Discard the monotonous tune of iron derived from meat. A plethora of iron-rich options are available in the plant kingdom, each with distinct strengths and flavor profiles:

Leafy Greens: Let collard, kale, and spinach take center stage! Iron champions, these leafy powerhouses pack a serious punch of this essential mineral.

Lentils and Beans: Beans, the unsung heroes of the plant-based world, are powerful sources of protein as well as dependable allies. Black beans, lentils, chickpeas—the list is endless and offers scrumptious and varied ways to increase your intake of iron.

Nuts and seeds: Don't undervalue these minuscule but mighty nutritional powerhouses. Rich in iron, cashews, sesame seeds, and pumpkin seeds give your meals and snacks a satisfying crunch.

Tempeh and Tofu: These miracles made of soy are not only excellent sources of iron, but they can also absorb iron from other plant-based foods when cooked with them. They are not just protein replacements.

Fruits and Vegetables: The supporting cast should not be overlooked! Fruits high in vitamin C, such as oranges, bell peppers, and strawberries, can improve the way that iron is absorbed from other plant sources.

Bringing Your Plant-Based Iron Symphony into Harmony:

On a stage made of plants, creating a colorful iron symphony takes some orchestration:

Variety is the Key: Avoid becoming stale! Discover the wide variety of plant-based foods that are high in iron, try out new recipes, and maintain a healthy balance of iron and taste buds.

Power of Pairing: Recall that synergy is crucial! To optimize absorption, pair vitamin C-rich fruits and vegetables with iron-rich plant foods. Imagine lentil soup with a squeeze of lemon or spinach with orange segments.

Taking Care When Cooking: Some cooking techniques can prevent the absorption of iron. Steer clear of techniques like grilling or frying, which can affect iron bioavailability, and instead use gentle steaming, simmering, or stir-frying.

Pay Attention to Your Body: Observe how your body reacts to various sources of iron derived from plants. It's possible that some people absorb iron from specific foods more readily than others. Try different things to see what suits you the best.

Beyond the Plate: Iron Harmony's Supporting Acts:

Even though there are plenty of delectable plant-based options, keep in mind that iron absorption is a complicated drama with numerous supporting characters:

Hydration: Water conducts all biological functions, including the absorption of iron. Eight glasses of water a day should be the goal for the best possible iron transport and utilization.

Exercise: Iron metabolism is choreographed by movement. Frequent exercise improves blood flow and oxygen delivery, which facilitates the uptake and utilization of iron.

Stress management: Prolonged stress may cause problems absorbing iron. Maintaining your iron symphony in tune can be achieved by engaging in relaxation exercises like yoga, meditation, and deep breathing.

Consultation is Essential: See your healthcare provider if you have any concerns regarding your iron levels. They are able to evaluate your requirements, offer tailored advice, and rule out any underlying medical issues.

Boosting Your Iron Symphony of Plants:

Choosing plant-based iron options is about empowering your health and wellbeing, not just about diet. You can turn the murmurs of iron deficiency into a thriving symphony of vigor, energy, and resilience by implementing these tactics. Recall that you are the leader of your own health orchestra, and one of the most potent instruments in your toolkit is plant-based iron. So take the initiative, investigate the wide range of iron-rich options, and create a masterpiece of health powered by plants!

Open the curtains on your iron symphony of plants and listen to the empowering tune of wellbeing!

- ## Overcoming Myths and Misconceptions about Iron in Plant Foods

Dispelling Myths and Misconceptions about Iron in Plant Foods: Demystifying the Plant Plate We are a symphony of energy conducted by iron, the maestro of oxygen in our cells. However, a lot of people doubt the efficacy of plant-based sources of this essential mineral because they are frequently surrounded by myths and false information. Do not be afraid, fellow devotees of health! By dispelling myths and correcting misconceptions, this guide will provide you with the knowledge you need to confidently navigate the plant-based iron landscape.

Myth 1: Iron from plants is not as good as iron from animals.

This strikes a loud false note. Even though heme iron derived from animal sources has a slightly higher bioavailability, non-heme iron derived from plants is still easily absorbed by our bodies, particularly when combined with absorption-enhancing factors like vitamin C. Research has indicated that plant-based people can obtain sufficient iron levels in their diets if they choose their foods carefully and prepare them properly.

Myth #2: The only plant-based source of iron is leafy greens.

Though leafy greens such as kale and spinach are iron champions, they are not the main attraction! Good sources of non-heme iron include lentils, beans, chickpeas, tofu, tempeh, nuts, seeds, and even some fruits and vegetables like potatoes and dried apricots. They also add a variety of flavors and textures to your plant-based symphony.

Myth #3: Plant-based iron is destroyed by cooking.

This isn't totally true. Iron bioavailability can be slightly decreased by some cooking techniques, but it can also be increased by others! While grilling and frying can affect the amount of iron in food, gentle steaming, simmering, and stir-frying are your friends. Furthermore, it has been demonstrated that some spices, such as black pepper and turmeric, enhance the absorption of iron.

Myth #4: Iron deficiency resulting from plants is unavoidable.

There is an easy way to refute this misconception. Because non-heme iron has a lower bioavailability, people who follow a plant-based diet may be slightly more susceptible to iron deficiency. However, iron deficiency can be effectively prevented and managed with a balanced, diverse plant-based diet, appropriate food preparation techniques, and adequate vitamin C intake.

Myth #5: The only way to treat a plant-based iron deficiency is with iron supplements.

Although iron supplements may provide a short-term fix in specific circumstances, they shouldn't be the first line of treatment. The initial focus should be on addressing any underlying causes of iron deficiency, optimizing absorption with vitamin C and other factors, and prioritizing dietary sources of iron. Use of supplements should only be done so under a doctor's supervision.

The Melodic Symphony of Iron Derived from Plants:

You can create a vibrant symphony of health and well-being by dispelling these myths and embracing the diverse world of plant-based iron sources.

These are important things to keep in mind:

Variety is essential. Investigate a variety of plant foods high in iron to make sure your body receives the complete complement of nutrients and minerals.

Pairing has great power: To optimize absorption, pair vitamin C-rich fruits and vegetables with iron-rich foods.

Cooking is important: Use mild cooking techniques and add spices that increase the bioavailability of iron.

Pay attention to your body. Keep an eye on your iron intake and energy levels. If you have any concerns, speak with your healthcare provider.

Honor the decisions you've made: Accept the deliciousness and health advantages of a plant-based diet and know that you are contributing to the well-being of the environment as well as your own health.

Recall that it is up to you to set the stage for ideal iron health. One nutritious bite at a time, you can create a masterpiece of well-being by busting myths and welcoming the varied melody of plant-based iron sources. Now go ahead and lead your own iron symphony powered by plants and feel the bright harmony of health!

Lift the curtain on your plant-based iron journey and see how a delicious, varied diet and wise decisions can change your life!

- **From Soil to Calm: Establishing Trust in a Plant-Based Iron Supplement**

Iron, the master of oxygen, gives our blood its red hue and powers all of our activities. However, the bright promise of this lifestyle can be overshadowed by whispers of iron deficiency for many, particularly for those starting a plant-based journey. Trailblazers who are concerned about their health need not worry! This manual serves as your compass, pointing the way toward a sure step toward iron sufficiency derived from plants.

Comprehending the Iron Landscape:

Let's demystify the terrain first. Non-heme iron, or iron derived from plants, is more difficult to absorb than heme iron, which is easily absorbed from animal sources. But fear not—this does not imply that the feat is unachievable! You can turn those doubtful rumblings into a confident chorus of iron sufficiency by knowing what influences absorption.

The Multifaceted Orchestra of Iron from Plants:

Similar to how a symphony comes to life with a variety of instruments, your plant-based iron requires a colorful orchestra of foods high in nutrients:

Leafy Greens: With their remarkable iron content, kale, spinach, and collard greens are the iron champions.

Legumes: Chickpeas, lentils, and beans are not only excellent sources of protein but also powerful allies of iron. Consider filling salads, stews, and curries.

Nuts and Seeds: Packed full of iron, zinc, and other vital minerals, these tiny titans are mighty. Add them to smoothies and salads, or just eat them as a nutritious snack.

Tempeh and tofu: These adaptable soy-based marvels are excellent for marinades, stir-fries, and scrambles because they easily absorb iron from other plant-based foods.

Rich in vitamin C Fruits and Vegetables: Consider strawberries, bell peppers, and oranges. These colorful allies improve the absorption of nonheme iron, enabling your iron orchestra to sing.

Enhancing Your Iron Symphony Made of Plants:

Here's how to improve the harmony of your plant-based iron symphony beyond just adding these iron-rich players:

Variety Is Essential: Avoid being a one-hit wonder! Keep your meals and iron levels interesting by experimenting with the wide variety of iron-rich options available.

The Influence of Combining: The conductor of iron absorption is vitamin C. To enhance the absorption of iron, combine foods high in iron with bell peppers, citrus fruits, or even just a squeeze of lemon.

Taking Care When Cooking: Some cooking techniques, such as low-steam steaming or simmering, help retain iron content. Steer clear of harsh cooking techniques like grilling or frying as they may reduce the food's bioavailability.

Pay Attention to Your Body: Keep an eye on your general wellbeing and energy levels. For a customized assessment, speak with your healthcare provider if you have any concerns regarding your iron status.

Boosting Your Plant-Based Adventure:

Remember that knowledge, awareness, and a good dose of self-compassion are the keys to feeling confident in your plant-based approach to meeting your iron needs:

Appreciate Little Victories: Every bite of iron-rich food is a step closer to sufficiency. No matter how tiny, acknowledge and celebrate your progress.

Accept the Plenty: Iron-rich plant-based options abound in the plant-based world. Find joy in the journey and place your attention on the abundance rather than the limitations.

Seek Support: Don't be afraid to get in touch with other people who share your beliefs and medical professionals. Their advice and support can be very helpful to you as you embark on your plant-based journey.

Never forget that you are the conductor: Your wellbeing and general health are under your control. Make wise decisions, follow your gut, and take pleasure in the colorful symphony that is a plant-based lifestyle.

So confidently take the stage on your plant-based journey! Equipped with understanding, consciousness, and a hint of empathy for yourself, you can turn those murmurs of steely uncertainty into a thunderous chorus of wellbeing. Recall that you are the conductor of your own health symphony, and that one of the most potent instruments in your arsenal is plant-based iron. Lead the way, create a work of iron sufficiency art, and witness the life-changing potential of a plant-powered lifestyle!

Let going plant-based be an occasion to celebrate life, health, and all that nature has to offer!

- **Building a Future Symphony: A Harmonious Dance Between Sustainability and Health**

Imagine living in a world where vibrant communities are supported by verdant landscapes, where the sound of renewable energy permeates the atmosphere, and where sustainable practices are the ideal source of health. This is not a utopian dream; rather, it is the harmonious vision of a future that we can direct, one in which health and sustainability work together to build a thriving, resilient world for future generations.

The Prelude: Recognizing the Intertwined Threads

The intricate relationship that exists between environmental health and human well-being weaves our planet like a delicate tapestry. We ruin this tapestry and endanger our own well-being when we overuse resources, degrade ecosystems, and ignore ecological balance.

Unsustainable practices have resulted in climate change, which has a significant impact on human health. Severe weather conditions jeopardize access to clean water and food, and air pollution makes respiratory conditions worse. Vulnerable communities bear a disproportionate amount of the consequences, exacerbating social inequality and impeding the advancement of global health equity.

However, hidden within this discord is a potent harmony just waiting to be revealed. Sustainable practices are the foundation of a healthier future; they go beyond simple environmental remedies, such as organic farming, renewable energy, and responsible waste management.

The Initial Effort: Planting the Foundation of Sustainability

This symphony's opening movement starts with a mental shift. We need to shift from a consumption paradigm to a co-creation paradigm, where we honor the planet's boundaries and cooperate with its natural cycles. This is reflected in the decisions we make on a daily basis, such as choosing organic, locally grown produce or adopting energy-saving devices and consuming with awareness.

The stage must be set by governments through the implementation of laws that penalize polluters and encourage sustainable behavior. Not only are sustainable agriculture, renewable energy infrastructure, and vital ecosystems to be protected, but they are also investments in the health and well-being of future generations.

The Second Movement: Building Healthy Foundations

The foundation of a healthy future is provided by sustainable food systems. This entails giving organic farming methods—which improve soil health, safeguard biodiversity, and use fewer toxic chemicals—priority. It entails helping regional farmers, creating robust food systems, and guaranteeing that everyone has fair access to wholesome food.

A thriving planet is correlated with healthier eating choices. We can feed our bodies and lessen our impact on the environment by adopting plant-based diets, cutting down on food waste, and encouraging mindful consumption.

The Third Movement: Creating Cooperation Bridges

A global orchestra, comprising diverse communities coming together to compose a shared future, is needed for this symphony. Collaboration is the key to bridging divides, from young activists demanding climate action to indigenous communities protecting their ancestral knowledge of sustainable practices.

It is imperative to empower communities, encourage knowledge exchange, and support inclusive decision-making in order to guarantee that the advantages of sustainable practices are felt worldwide. It is imperative that we elevate one another's voices, give voice to underrepresented viewpoints, and acknowledge the synergistic effect of collaboration.

A Revelry of Health

Let us imagine a world where pure air fills our lungs, vibrant ecosystems teeming with life, and health and well-being flourish alongside a thriving planet as the last notes of this symphony resonate. This is the crescendo of a future we can design, note by note, decision by decision; it is not a far-off dream.

Allow us to be the generation leading this change in orchestration. Take up the instruments of sustainability, speak up for a healthier Earth, and work together to create a symphony of well-being for everybody. Recall that we create the future, not that it is something we inherit. Thus, let us foster a future in which health and sustainability coexist peacefully, creating a lively tune that will be remembered for many generations.

Let's work together to compose a future symphony in which every note exalts a thriving human race and a healthy planet.

Conclusion

The Grand Finale: Creating the Ideal Concluding Statement

A conclusion is a piece's last flourish, the melody that reverberates long after the last note disappears. Your work comes together and leaves a lasting impression on your audience at the curtain call, grand finale, or summation. However, writing a truly memorable ending can sometimes resemble negotiating a dramatic maze. Do not be alarmed, fellow writers! With the help of this guide, you will be able to write conclusions that captivate readers and leave them wanting more.

Recognizing the Effect of Closure:

A compelling conclusion accomplishes more than just restating your main ideas.

It is an effective tool for:

Strengthen your main point: The conclusion is your opportunity to emphasize the most important lesson from your work and make a lasting impact on the minds of your audience.

Inspire reflection, rethinking, or even action from your readers: A strong conclusion can evoke strong feelings in your audience and motivate them to act on your advice.

Give your readers a sense of closure and satisfaction: A well-written ending ties up any loose ends and gives your readers a sense of fulfillment.

Selecting the Appropriate Note:

Just as distinctive as the work itself is the flawless ending. The type of work you're doing, who your audience is, and the results you hope to achieve will all determine the best strategy.

Here are some typical conclusion types to take into account:

The Summary: This method ensures clarity and leaves no loose ends hanging by succinctly summarizing the key ideas of your work.

The Urgency to Act: A compelling conclusion forces your audience to act, whether it's through advocacy, more study, or introspection.

The Open Ending: This provocative conclusion invites readers to draw their own conclusions and carry on the discussion by leaving them considering the implications of your work.

The Appealing Emotion: An effective anecdote or vivid image can evoke strong feelings in your audience and have a long-lasting emotional effect.

Creating Your Magnum Opus:

Whatever kind of conclusion you decide on, the following universal components can increase its impact:

Clarity and conciseness: Steer clear of digressing or adding unneeded details. Make sure your conclusion is clear and concise.

Variety and rhythm: To keep your readers interested and prevent monotony, use a variety of sentence structures and figurative language.

Memorable language: A strong metaphor, a well-chosen quote, or a concluding sentence with resonance can make an impact.

A dash of individuality: Allow your distinct voice to come through! A sincere and real ending will help you establish a stronger connection with your audience.

Recall that the end is an essential component of your work and should not be treated as an afterthought. Your conclusions can become grand finales that leave your audience gasping in anticipation of your next masterpiece by knowing its power, picking the appropriate note, and carefully crafting it.

So, wordsmiths, go forth! Write endings that sing, linger, and pique the interest of your readers. Never forget that you own the stage and have the ability to pull off the ideal conclusion.

Appendix

Plant-Based Iron-Rich Symphony: Tasty Recipes to Boost Your Health

Within us, iron, the oxygen conductor in our cells, creates a dynamic energy symphony. Although a lot of people think that iron is only found in meat, there are a lot of different iron-rich plant options available that can create tasty and nourishing meals for you. So, give up on dietary restrictions and harness the power of plant-based iron by preparing these motivating, high-iron recipes!

Breakfast Symphony:

Spiced Lentil Scramble: A powerful source of iron and protein to start your day. Add the cumin, turmeric, and garam masala after sautéing the chopped onions and peppers. Finally, crumble in the cooked lentils. To add a creamy touch, garnish with a dollop of plain yogurt and a sprinkle of chopped cilantro.

Berry-Spinach Smoothie: Packed full of iron and vitamin C, this smoothie is a powerful energy booster. For a burst of nutrition and refreshment, blend spinach, frozen berries, banana, almond milk, and squeeze of lemon.

Iron-Fortified Oatmeal: Drizzle tahini, chia seeds, and hemp seeds over your oatmeal to give it an extra boost. This combo provides you with an iron and complete protein source to keep you going throughout the morning.

Lunchtime Concerto:

Black bean burgers: These plant-based patties are not only incredibly tasty but also incredibly strong. Add cooked quinoa, chopped walnuts, cumin, and smoked paprika to mashed black beans. Make into patties and bake or pan-fry for a hearty, high-iron lunch option.

This filling soup can be made in just one pot with lentils and leafy greens. Add lentils, sautéed onions and garlic, and your preferred leafy greens, such as spinach or kale, to the vegetable broth. Once softened, savor the dish with some crusty bread for dipping

.

Tofu Scramble infused with ginger: Accept the flexibility of tofu! Combine it with finely chopped veggies, nutritional yeast, turmeric, and a small amount of soy sauce in a pan. This iron- and protein-rich scramble is great on its own or in tacos or wraps.

A serenade for dinner:

A plant-based take on a classic comfort food: lentil shepherd's pie. For a filling and iron-rich supper, try substituting cooked lentils and mushrooms for the ground meat, topping with creamy mashed potatoes, and baking until golden brown.

Stir-fried Tofu with Vegetables: Packed full of flavor and iron, this dish is simple and quick to prepare. Tofu cubes are stir-fried with bell peppers, broccoli, and other favorite vegetables in a tasty sauce made with soy sauce, ginger, and garlic.

Curry made with coconut and chickpeas: this aromatic curry is very delicious. Add the curry powder, garlic powder, and onions to a sauté pan. Add the chickpeas, coconut milk, and vegetables. Serve with brown rice for a satisfying and savory dinner.

Sweets for the Aftershow:

Chocolate with Iron Fortification: Savor a guilt-free indulgence! To enhance your iron intake, select dark chocolate with a high cocoa percentage and enjoy it as a filling, antioxidant-rich snack with berries or nuts.

Personalized Trail Mix: Combine nuts, seeds, dried fruit, and chunks of dark chocolate to make your own iron-packed mix. This is the ideal on-the-go snack to maintain your iron stores and energy levels.

Berries and Chia Pudding: This is a simple dessert to make and is high in protein and iron. For a nutritious and filling treat, soak chia seeds in almond milk for the entire night. Then, garnish with fresh berries and a dollop of maple syrup.

Recall that diversity is essential! Try these recipes and play around with various plant-based ingredients to make your own delicious, iron-rich symphony. Remember to complement your meals with fruits and vegetables high in vitamin C to enhance iron absorption and realize the full nutritional benefits of a plant-based diet.

One tasty bite at a time, you can create a masterpiece of health and well-being by diving into the colorful world of plant-based iron. So conductor, pick up your culinary baton and start this iron-rich symphony of plant-based recipes!

- **Iron Symphony: A Category-Based Guide to Food Sources**

A vibrant symphony of energy is conducted within us by iron, the maestro of oxygen in our cells. To really shine, though, it needs the right instruments, just like any conductor. This guide will help you create a masterpiece of iron sufficiency in your diet by taking you through the varied orchestra of foods rich in iron, categorized for your convenience.

Seafood, poultry, and meats:

These are the traditional iron giants, providing easily assimilated heme iron:

Red Meat: Iron-rich foods include liver, pig, lamb, and beef. To retain the iron content, select lean cuts and cook them by grilling, baking, or stewing.

Poultry: Especially dark meat, chicken, turkey, and duck are excellent providers of iron. For a healthier option, go for skinless varieties.

Seafood: Scallops, mussels, oysters, and clams are examples of iron champion shellfish. Sardines, salmon, and tuna are also excellent choices for fish.

Beans and Legumes:

These superfoods made of plants are very strong in non-heme iron, but their absorption is a little bit lower:

Lentils: These adaptable beans have a variety of colors and are high in fiber, protein, and iron.

Kidney beans: Ideal for stews, soups, and chili, these beans are high in iron.

Black beans are an excellent source of iron, protein, and antioxidants and are a common ingredient in many cuisines.

Chickpeas: A versatile legume, they can be added to salads and curries, roasted, or mashed into hummus.

Grains, Nuts, and Seeds:

These supporting cast members give your nutritional symphony a dash of iron:

Pumpkin Seeds: Rich in magnesium, zinc, and iron, pumpkin seeds make a tasty and wholesome snack.

Sesame Seeds: Plentiful and nutritious, these seeds are high in iron, calcium, and good fats.

Quinoa: This grain, which is high in protein, has a reasonable amount of iron. If you want an added boost, go for fortified varieties.

Tempeh and tofu: These soy-based foods are great meat substitutes since they're high in protein and iron.

Produce and Fruits:

Even though they aren't the biggest providers of iron, some fruits and vegetables can help meet your daily requirements:

Leafy Greens: For better absorption, spinach, kale, and collard greens are great sources of iron. They also work well when combined with foods high in vitamin C.

Fruits that are Dehydrated: Raisins, prunes, and apricots are high in iron and fiber, but watch out for their sugar content.

Potatoes are a versatile vegetable that are high in iron and can be prepared in a variety of ways.

Extra Instruments: Spices and Vitamin C:

Recall that the following elements can improve iron absorption:

Vitamin C: Tomatoes, bell peppers, and citrus fruits all increase the absorption of non-heme iron. For maximum benefit, eat them with meals high in iron.

Spices: Studies have demonstrated that black pepper and turmeric enhance the absorption of iron. Add a pinch of spice to your food to enhance taste and facilitate iron absorption.

Putting Your Iron Symphony Together:

You can make your diet a colorful, iron-rich symphony for your health by including these varied food sources.

Here are a few more pointers:

Variety is essential. Never rely just on one or two sources of iron. Examine the variety of choices in each area to make sure you're getting enough in.

For power, pair: To optimize absorption, pair foods high in iron with foods high in vitamin C.

Cooking matters: Iron content can be impacted by specific cooking techniques. To preserve iron, use gentle methods such as simmering or steaming.

Pay attention to your body. Keep an eye on your iron levels and energy levels. Should you have any concerns regarding an iron deficiency, speak with your healthcare provider.

Recall that creating a diet rich in iron is a process rather than a final goal. Explore, try new things, and savor the mouthwatering symphony of opportunities presented by the plant and animal kingdoms. So grab a fork, maestro, and start creating your own iron-infused work of health and wellness!

- **Getting Ahead on the Nutritional Seas: A Handy Dictionary**

There are times when the vast ocean of nutrition feels overwhelming, full of terms that resemble mysterious messages from another planet. But fear not, brave explorers of health! This glossary acts as your reliable compass, helping you navigate the confusing waters of dietary jargon and arrive at a clear comprehension of the terms that influence your overall health. Now, put on your figurative life jacket and let's get started!

The macronutrients consist of three main components: proteins, lipids, and carbohydrates. They supply the majority of our energy and are vital to many body processes.

Our main source of energy, carbohydrates can be found in both simple **(sugars)** and complex **(whole grains, fruits, and vegetables)** forms.

Select complex carbohydrates for fiber and long-lasting energy.

Don't be afraid of fat! For the proper functioning of cells, hormone regulation, and nutrient absorption, healthy fats such as those in nuts, avocados, and olive oil are essential. Reduce your intake of processed foods' harmful trans and saturated fats.

Proteins: The building blocks of life, proteins are necessary for immune system support, muscle growth and repair, and enzyme function. Pick lean protein sources such as lentils, beans, and fish.

Micronutrients: Your health will sail smoothly thanks to these vital vitamins and minerals, which are like the small but powerful crew of your nutritional ship.

Vitamins: These organic substances, which include vitamins A, C, and D, are essential for a number of body processes. They are available in two forms: water soluble **(B vitamins, C)** and fat soluble **(A, D, E, and K).**

Minerals: Strong bones, healthy blood, and normal nerve function depend on these inorganic elements, which include calcium, iron, and magnesium.

Additional Crucial Words:

Calories: The food's energy unit. Aim for a daily calorie intake that is balanced according to your activity level and specific needs.

Fiber: This food ingredient promotes gut health and aids in digestion. Select meals high in fiber, such as whole grains, fruits, and vegetables.

The Glycemic Index **(GI)** gauges the rate at which food elevates blood sugar levels. Choose low-GI foods for long-lasting energy and fullness.

Saturated fat: This type of fat, which is present in processed foods and animal products, can raise cholesterol and increase the risk of heart disease. Don't take too much in.

The worst fat in the food world is trans fat, which is present in processed foods and can lead to heart disease and other health issues. Steer clear of it like a pirate clears a storm!

A waxy substance produced by the liver and present in certain foods is cholesterol. Cholesterol comes in **"good"** and **"bad"** varieties. Reduce LDL **("bad")** cholesterol and increase HDL **("good")** cholesterol levels.

Recall that there is much more to nutrition than this glossary. Continue learning and picking up new terms as you delve deeper into the wide world of nutrition and health so that you can make decisions that are best for your health. Good food, my fellow explorers!

I hope your journey through nutrition is full of clear understanding, tasty discoveries, and a good dose of curiosity. And never forget that the component that ignites your desire for a vibrant and healthy life is always the most crucial one on your plate!

- **Getting Around in the Nutritional Maze: A List of Trusted Sources**

With so much information available and sometimes contradicting guidance, the field of nutrition can have the feel of a dense jungle. But fear not, brave adventurers in health! This guide gives you a strong compass and points you in the direction of trustworthy resources so you can confidently travel the route to optimal well-being.

Websites run by the government:

National Institutes of Health (NIH): A wealth of evidence-based information on a range of health issues, including nutrition, can be found on the NIH website. Examine their Dietary Guidelines for Americans, investigate particular nutrients, or read up on the most recent findings in research.

Food and Drug Administration (FDA) of the United States: The FDA website offers reliable information on nutrition labeling, dietary supplements, and food safety. Use their Food Facts label database, pick up tips for eating well, or keep up with safety alerts and food recalls.

USDA FoodData Central: This extensive database offers calories, macronutrients, micronutrients, and food components along with comprehensive nutritional information on thousands of foods. Utilize it to investigate particular ingredients, keep track of your intake, or compare food options.

Expert Associations:

The Academy of Nutrition and Dietetics **(AND)** provides evidence-based resources on healthy eating, managing chronic conditions, and nutrition on its website. Locate a licensed dietitian nearby, read through their consumer-friendly publications, or view their position papers on a range of subjects.

American Heart Association (AHA): The AHA website offers helpful advice on heart-healthy eating. Discover the DASH diet, look through recipe ideas, and locate tools for controlling blood pressure and cholesterol with food.

American Diabetes Association (ADA): A wealth of information about eating well to manage diabetes can be found on the ADA website. Get advice on meal planning, look through resources on carb counting, and view their most recent research findings.

Dependable media sources

The esteemed Harvard T.H. Chan School of Public Health provides a plethora of evidence-based materials on nutrition and wellness. Visit their Nutrition Source page for comprehensive articles, research summaries, and helpful advice on eating a healthy diet.

The Well Section of the New York Times: Well-researched articles on a range of health-related topics, including nutrition, are available from this reliable source. Learn about the most recent research findings, find wholesome recipes, and acquire professional advice.

Journal of Medicine in Britain (BMJ): Research articles on a range of health-related subjects, including nutrition, are published in this reputable medical publication. Read their open-access articles to learn more about particular subjects in-depth, keep up with the most recent findings, and get advice from world experts.

Applications and Web Resources:

MyPlate: This app, created by the USDA, assists you in customizing your meal selections according to your dietary requirements and calorie requirements. Create wholesome meal plans, monitor your consumption, and establish objectives for your dietary journey.

Cronometer: This all-inclusive app helps you monitor your consumption of macronutrients, micronutrients, and different food components by offering thorough nutrient breakdowns for thousands of foods. Excellent for people looking for granular nutritional analysis or for those with particular dietary needs.

Fooducate: This app scans food labels with the camera on your smartphone and provides comprehensive nutritional data instantly. On the go, research ingredients, contrast brands, and make wise decisions.

Recall that the critical eye is essential. Consider the information's source, give priority to resources with supporting data, and steer clear of advice that lacks evidence or is sensationalized. Have faith in your instincts, seek the advice of licensed medical professionals when necessary, and relish the adventure of learning about the fascinating realm of nutrition!

So, seize your figurative machete and set out on your dietary journey! You can make your way through the informational maze with this guide and a healthy dose of curiosity, emerging with the knowledge and self-assurance you need to fuel your body and thrive. Recall that the most fulfilling discoveries are frequently made off the beaten path, so never stop learning, growing, and igniting your desire for a long, healthy life!

Made in the USA
Monee, IL
27 March 2024

55891b2e-ceb2-4d2e-bc91-713c8dd1bf47R01